INNOVATION
without
RENOVATION
in the elementary school

Dr. Richard J. Morton
Principal, Greenwood Elementary School
Cherry Creek School District,
Arapahoe County, Colorado

Jane Morton
Teacher-Writer

CITATION PRESS ❖ NEW YORK ❖ 1974

To the Children

Acknowledgements

The authors wish to express their appreciation to Dr. Carol McCallum, who wrote much of the counseling proposal that was submitted to the school board, to the Greenwood staff, past and present, the Cherry Creek School System, and to all of our friends whose help and support made this book possible.

◇ DICK AND JANE

CONTENTS

❖❖❖❖❖

FOREWORD

I ONCE MADE, AT LEAST THOUGHT I MADE, A PARTICULARLY brilliant speech on the need to humanize the schooling process. I spoke with the tongue of an angel about our sins of commission and omission. I talked about openness and nongradedness, about renewal and renovation, about perceiving and accepting, about positive self-images and schools without failure and, in short, every worthwhile and appealing idea I had or ever heard. The audience loved it. After a prolonged and warming applause, I asked for questions from the listeners.

The first principal who spoke put my presentation in a different perspective. He said, "I liked what you said and I enjoyed the clever ways you expressed yourself, but I already knew everything you talked about and I believe in what you are preaching as firmly as you do yourself. Would you like to change places? I'll make the speeches, and you go to my school and reorganize it. It's not that I don't want to change—I just don't know where to begin."

That nameless principal was on target. Educators have the vocabulary of change. The problem is not what do we believe—it is how do we do it. I wish on that occasion that I could have referred him to *Innovation Without Renovation in the Elementary School.*

The work the Mortons have produced delights me for a number of reasons. Unlike my speech, the book goes right to the heart of the matter. There is no "Historical Perspective," no "Philosophical Orientation," no "Contemporary Social Setting." Their innovation is to recognize that such chapters, while valuable, already exist in abundance. They have openly and unashamedly written a how-to-do-it book for people who are already convinced and are ready to get on with the job.

However, do not make the mistake of thinking that because this is a practical handbook, it suffers from an inadequate philosophical base. The authors have wisely chosen to use descriptions and illustrations rather than inanimate precepts. The sound pedological orientation is here, but it is woven through the suggestions rather than served on a platter like John the Baptist's head.

I also like the cafeteria approach. There is something here for every taste. Big ideas and small tricks abound throughout the manuscript. The reader may take a light snack or a full meal. The presentation is unified and comprehensive and is intended to help change the entire elementary school. However, the ideas stand alone, and some may be used while others may be ignored. Equally important, after a basic presentation, alternatives and variations are suggested for many innovations.

And finally I can recommend *Innovation Without Renovation in the Elementary School* because it recognizes that openness isn't an organization, it's a state of mind. It avoids ever suggesting that simply removing walls or rearranging desks can change a school. But if the school personnel are ready to find better ways, they will find them here.

William L. Pharis
Executive Director
National Association of
Elementary School Principals
April 1974

❖❖❖❖❖❖❖❖❖❖❖❖❖❖❖❖❖

INNOVATION
without
RENOVATION

INTRODUCTION

A TRADITIONALLY ORIENTED PRINCIPAL, OPPOSED TO ALMOST all innovations, leafed through the program at an educational convention. When he came to the topic "Free the Children," he flipped the program closed. "Free the children!" he exclaimed in disbelief. "Why, they're running amuk now!"

But it was to free the children imprisoned in traditional programs where they either passed, failed, or were something called average, where they slept through lectures and marched through halls, where one answered a question while twenty-nine were silent, that innovative educators sought to change the system. When the whole democratic process depends on educated citizens who think for themselves, schools that still measure their success by the number of students who adapt, adjust, and conform, cannot be the answer for our children or our country.

For many, open space seemed to promise what they thought schools with walls could not—freedom—freedom to move and mingle, to question and explore, even to make mistakes; freedom to be the individuals they are and to go as far as their potential will take them.

Administrators planning a new school or remodeling an old one have a chance to opt for open space, but what of those who have an old building with no funds to remodel? Must they pass up new teaching techniques and opportunities to do the best they can for individual children while they retain the goals and values they have always had because of building limitations?

We believe they don't have to, for it isn't space that makes the difference—it's the staff. Traditional programs go on in open space schools, and open programs go on in schools with walls. Although you may want to tear down a wall or two for a larger instructional area, you do not need to gut the school building before you try team teaching, a continuous progress program, or media centers.

Most innovative programs can be put into effect in schools with walls. This isn't far-out theory. We have implemented new programs at Greenwood, an elementary school with walls, and we have seen them work. There is freedom with responsibility in the classrooms, more creativity than conformity in teachers and pupils, and a friendly happy attitude prevailing throughout the school. If the children are running amuk, we aren't aware of it.

Open space advocates argue that open space with carpets and color provides a more natural setting for learning. They cite the learning alternatives and individualized instruction that can be offered in their schools without walls. We contend all of this is possible in a traditional building. In fact, John Coe, a noted English primary school educator, visited our school and commented that we had open space within walls.

To date no studies have been made that prove that all students function better without walls. It is not the walls but the concepts that are important. No walls can lead to problems that don't exist within conventional classrooms, such as wanting to show a movie to a small group and having no way to darken just one corner of a large open space room; and no matter how much acoustical tile or how much carpeting is installed, there are still some group activities that are disturbing to other groups in one big open area.

An innovative superintendent may encourage change in a district, but if *meaningful* change is to take place within a school, it has to come through the principal. Principals bring about change in their schools the same way teachers bring about change in their classrooms—they involve those involved. They also make sure that teachers have freedom, freedom to try and to succeed or fail.

Such a statement as, "We have an old school, so we can't do any of the new things," is an excuse behind which educators who don't want to change hide. For instance, if you think a good teacher is the one with straight rows of desks and chairs, a quiet class, and a clean floor, if you want the halls silent except at passing time, and if you believe test scores somewhere around the national average tell you how well your school is doing, you may not be limited so much by walls as by your attitude.

If you believe you can't make changes, you can't. It is easier to do nothing. But if you realize that as a professional educator it is your highest responsibility to provide what you believe is the best learning situation for your students, if you instill in your teachers a caring attitude and an enthusiasm to try something new, if you believe you can make things happen, you can.

I am the principal of an elementary school in the Cherry Creek School District, an area of approximately ninety-five square miles and encompassing several cities and villages southeast of Denver, Colorado. Greenwood is a traditional school as far as the building goes, but in no way are we educating our six hundred suburban students the way we were fifteen years ago when the building was new. Then we had self-contained classrooms, graded report cards, a textbook approach to teaching most subjects, and no counseling program, and the principal and the central office made most of the decisions. Now we have team teaching and team planning; we have report forms that describe what the child has learned; we use a multi-media approach; we have a total school library program, more teacher decision-making, and a full-time elementary counselor as well as a program for children with learning disabilities.

We didn't make changes just because we wanted to try something new. We made changes to meet needs. We asked questions: Will it make a difference? Will it improve skills or build self-concepts? Will it help the child continue to learn as eagerly as he did when he entered school?

Once we decided to make changes, we had to make decisions about what direction the changes would take. There are so many new directions in education that educators are confused. They wonder which way to go. No one knows for sure which way is the right way, so there was no one to tell us. It would have been easy to branch off in too many directions at once, so we developed plans for innovations that seemed right for us and stayed with them long enough to see if they worked.

Some of the suggestions we propose and plans we suggest have worked at our school; some at other schools. We are saying, "This is a way, but not the *only* way to go." Our school and our district do not have all the answers. We are still learning. We are fortunate in having an administration that encourages change, a staff willing to try something new, and parents who cooperate with the changes we want to make.

Throughout this book we refer to traditionally built schools. When we do this, we realize that we are speaking of schools that range in age from seventy-five years to less than a year and that there are great differences among them. There are more options open in the newer schools with wider halls, adequate electrical outlets, and larger rooms than there are in the older schools with dark narrow halls and one electric outlet at the front of small, crowded classrooms. Traditional schools are located in rural areas, the suburbs, and the central cities. Because of the differences in facilities and location, not all of our suggestions will apply to every school. Use what you can, adapt where you can, and change what you will. This book was written to show you how.

UTILIZING
EXISTING BUILDING SPACE
FOR A NEW PROGRAM

"Corners and Corridors"
❖❖❖❖

ON A BRIEF TRIP TO ENGLAND, A MAN ORDERED A SUIT FROM A British tailor. The suit needed alterations, so he left it overnight and returned for it the next day. When he went into the shop, he was handed a box that he didn't bother to open, as he had barely enough time to catch the train he was taking to the continent. He undressed, went to bed, and threw his old suit out the train window. The next morning he opened the box and discovered he had been given the wrong suit. The one in the box was a child's size ten.

This story points up the problems involved when you throw out the old before you are sure you have something better to take its place.

◆ PLANNING FOR CHANGE

Many of the innovations in education are good, but change for the sake of change in the schools isn't the answer. The staff working together should identify student and community needs and then make the changes that will better meet those needs.

When our staff makes a change, that change must first fill a need and then fit the philosophy the staff developed for the school. The Greenwood School philosophy states that:

◇ Each pupil is an individual and as such possesses the potentialities of making a desirable contribution to society.

◇ We share with the home and the community the responsibility for the development of character, as well as the moral and the ethical values which are fundamental to each child's education.

◇ We shall endeavor to help each child realize his greatest potential, to develop a love of learning, to think and act creatively, to achieve a sense of security and belonging, and to become a well-adjusted, self-directed, responsible member of an ever-changing society.

◇ Each member of the faculty team cooperates to assist the development of each child in terms of his mental, social, physical, and emotional growth.

◇ Each child is unique and possesses the potential to contribute at his level not only to his present but to his future world.

◇ The curriculum of the school is an integral part of the child's total experience.

◇ Teachers and parents share in the common responsibility of guiding the child toward a more positive direction—self-realization.

◇ The school is a major cultural center.

◇ Home and school are realistic partners in meeting the needs of all the children.

According to our philosophy, we believe in teaching the individual child. Throughout the nation there are many new programs to individualize instruction, but our staff decided that the Individually Guided Education Program developed at the University of Wisconsin best fit our philosophy and the organizational pattern we already had.

We will limit our discussion of IGE to school facilities in this chapter but will deal with the IGE concept in depth in Chapter XV.

The IGE organizational pattern calls for four major grouping modes:

1. The independent mode—Students work by themselves with tapes or films, with resource materials, or they read a book.

2. The one-to-one mode—Students work with an aide, a teacher, or another student on a one-to-one basis.

3. The small group mode—A group consisting of four to eleven students works together to achieve a common learning objective.

4. The large group mode—A class-size group or larger is brought together to see a film, a program, or to hear a speaker.

Changes we have made in space utilization were made to accommodate these grouping patterns.

◆ CREATING NEW INSTRUCTIONAL AREAS

Once you have identified a need and decided on a program, survey existing facilities outside as well as inside the school building. Look at space available with the idea of converting or rearranging to form new instructional areas.

Any large area standing idle during much of the school day might be converted to a new program. Ebert Elementary School in Denver is an old school with a traditional auditorium. The auditorium may be fancier than most, for it even has a balcony projection booth divided into three small rooms. For years the projection booth was used only for the purpose intended, the showing of films. Now the three small rooms, ideal space for small group reading instruction, are in constant use.

Using portable chalkboards for partitioning, the staff divided the main auditorium into instructional areas that are easily converted back to an auditorium when the need arises. Even the stage serves as an instructional area.

If auditorium chairs are fastened to the floor (those at

Ebert School are movable), there is less flexibility in such an arrangement, but using portable chalkboards and the aisles as natural divisions, new instructional areas are still possible.

To individualize instruction, it is desirable to create listening centers where students have access to cassette tapes, record players, and earphones. New schools build in listening centers; old schools must create them.

Sometimes space for a listening center is there but is being used for a different purpose. For instance, one typical elementary classroom had an adjoining coatroom five by six feet. Pegboard partitions five feet high separated it from the rest of the classroom. There was a doorway into the coatroom and shelves along the wall. This was a good spot for a listening area, but what to do with the coats was another problem. Although no adjoining hall space was available, the class agreed to use space down the hall and around a corner. The coat storage situation was worked out to everyone's satisfaction, and now the listening center is in full operation.

Often a rearrangement creates space. A team of five teachers decided to put one hundred twenty-five students into four classrooms instead of five. The team thought this was worthwhile, as it emptied a fifth room for a mini-media center that was open all day to the students in those classes under the supervision of one of the five teachers who had a master's degree in media.

In your quest for new instructional areas, look beyond the walls of the school to the possibilities of outdoor education. In a natural, informal outdoor setting, students can study anything from ecology to mathematics. Three four by eight foot redwood picnic tables will seat a classroom. The advantage of using the outdoors is that there is room to practically apply principles that students are learning. For instance, math students can measure the height of a building through triangulation, they can pace off an acre of ground, or they can measure the distance between two trees. Chapter XI offers more suggestions for using the outdoors in learning activities and gives specific advice on establishing an outdoor learning laboratory.

◆ USING THE HALLS FOR INSTRUCTION

It may be more difficult to change traditional concepts about the halls than to change the actual physical setup. One of these concepts, that of using the halls for discipline, should be thrown out with the trash. Halls are not a place to practice effective discipline, especially if the goal is to change unwanted behavior in a positive way. Another concept, that students should never be unsupervised in the halls is also wrong. Here students can learn responsibility that comes with being trusted to study when no one is watching. A third concept to overturn is that halls were built to serve as coat closets and traffic movers. They may have been once, but we need to look at them now in terms of space for instruction.

Utilize hall space that ordinarily receives little use for display purposes and instructional areas. In one older school the halls are an art gallery. Traveling displays on loan from the public library or the museum are constantly brought in to enrich the creative arts program. Some schools line their halls with art work exchanged with schools in other countries; some display student work. In other schools, science displays contribute to the instructional program.

A study carrel, a desk for one or two students, and/or a small rectangular table are all you need to turn parts of the hall into study areas for individual and small group learning.

In any hall in our building at any given hour, you might see a teacher's aide, a volunteer parent, or a high school student working with a small group, reinforcing what has been taught; two students giving individualized spelling lessons to each other; or children working individually, perhaps on a reading activity, perhaps on another project, while the rest of their class works with the classroom teacher.

Some schools are finding a place in the halls for a mini-media center containing a tape recorder, two or three individual film viewers, library books, a set of encyclopedias, picture sets, and 35mm slide sets. Cupboards and shelves for storage in the area make it easier to keep track of the equipment.

Using the halls even facilitates change. Open corridor plans vary, but basically they involve a group of four or five teachers whose rooms open onto the same corridor. The teachers use their own rooms as a home base and the corridor as a pipeline between the rooms and for common activities. The corridor connection seems to bring the teachers out of the isolation of their self-contained classroom and makes it easier for them to share interests and ideas and to interact with each other. Changes are not forced upon teachers but come about as a result of an arrangement that gives them a chance to grow.

It could be that fire department regulations, rather than traditional concepts, will limit your use of halls. Regulations vary with each fire department. Some have no stipulations concerning the halls; others allow chairs but no tables; while still others specifically prohibit all furniture. If no furniture is allowed and unless there is some other unusual rule, students could still sit against lockers or walls or on steps, with lapboards if necessary, to take advantage of the learning opportunities the halls afford.

◆ DEVELOPING LEARNING AREAS WITHIN THE CLASSROOM

Teachers can make physical changes within their classrooms that are as meaningful as any undertaken on a school-wide

12 ◆

basis. It takes more energy and imagination than money to replace rows of desks in old classrooms with individual stations and small group centers, but the results are worth the effort.

Children love cubbyholes, and teachers find many of them do better work when they have a place to go where they can be by themselves. Architects plan cubbyholes for new schools; teachers in old schools can build their own. In the process they become notorious scroungers. They will ask for anything, from old electric cable spools to grocery store displays. They cut open and decorate old cardboard refrigerator boxes, make small Indian tepees from old sheets and bamboo sticks, and build carrels from scraps of cardboard, plywood, or pegboard. They construct platforms, such as tree houses, from scrap lumber, of cardboard and fiberboard, or by stacking and bolting large cable spools together. Not only do the platforms provide additional space, children love to climb into them. Sometimes being able to reach that particular spot is a goal, the incentive they need to do good work. The booklet *Building with Tubes and Building with Cardboard* (Advisory for Open Education, 90 Sherman St., Cambridge, Mass. 02140; $.60) might be helpful to teachers and administrators seeking ways to construct new learning centers. The three illustrated booklets in the "Room to Learn" series by Joan Dean (*Working Space, Language Arts*, and *A Place to Paint*, New York: Citation Press, 1973, each $1.45) are also full of ideas for creating, saving, and utilizing space in an ordinary classroom.

Teachers can also arrange their furniture to gain the space they need for special purposes. Corners can be turned into study or media centers defined by small rugs and/or set off with movable bookshelves. Furniture can be grouped to accommodate two, three, four, or six students at a time, thereby creating small instructional areas throughout the room.

There are other possibilities. For example, furniture itself takes up room. By removing some desks and by organizing centers where children work at different times, teachers gain more space for creative use.

But no matter how you arrange or rearrange, convert or create, the end result should be a better learning situation; otherwise you might as well still have the suit that you threw out the window.

PREPARING THE STAFF FOR CHANGE

"So What If You Didn't Do It Last Year?"
❖❖❖❖❖

A TEACHER TOOK HER CLASS TO THE MUSEUM. AS THE CHILDREN walked through the building to the place where they were to begin their tour, a large sculpture caught their attention. They began to gather around and gaze at it. At that point the teacher moved them along by saying, "If you kids don't hurry up, you aren't going to see anything."

The point is that some teachers are afraid to change their plans regardless of opportunities that present themselves unexpectedly, just as they are afraid to change their methods of teaching regardless of the improvements a change might bring. When it comes to change, they are more concerned about what the change will do to them than about what it will do for their students.

The administrator's job, therefore, is to provide the leadership that will move the staff toward planned change. He should be a source of inspiration, but he must involve others in the decision-making process if the new program is to succeed. Meaningful, lasting changes in the schools come about when the innovation meets a need and when teachers have had a part in the planning and the implementation. Changes that result from administrative dictates are neither effective nor lasting.

For example, one large school district floated a bond issue for remodeling some of the older schools. After the issue passed, someone from the central administration was sent to survey the schools and to decide what needed doing. The teachers were bypassed completely. Consequently they feel they are stuck with projects they could have done without while they do without the projects they really wanted.

Bringing about change is not always easy, particularly in older schools. New schools start with new staffs—teachers transferring from other schools, teachers fresh from college, or teachers with various interim experiences. These people made a change when they joined the faculty of a new school. They don't know what's been done in the past, and they don't know each other. They are generally more willing to look at new ways of doing things than faculty who have been together in the same building for a number of years.

An older faculty may be set in their ways, comfortable and secure doing things the way they have done them for years. The teacher who, instead of having had ten different years of experience, has repeated one experience ten times, sees work involved with change. Even a teacher who does a fairly good job may not want to change, because she knows she is having some success now and isn't sure whether she would have as much under a new system.

Older faculty, by the way, does not refer to the age of individual faculty members. When it comes to trying innovations, age doesn't seem to make any difference. Some young teachers are less willing to change than teachers almost ready to retire. One older teacher, two years from retirement, for instance, had taught reading from one basic reader for over eighteen years. When we adopted a new reading program, she was one of the leaders in individualization.

Some teachers don't know why they don't want to change, but they say, "That's the way we've always done it," or "We did it this way last year." They have made up their minds,

"Paperbacks won't last," or "There will be too much confusion," or they have dire predictions of "What will happen if. . . ."

Before the dress code was finally dropped in one city school, the faculty discussed relaxing the code. There were forecasts of impending disaster. "If we let the girls wear long dresses, they will fall on the stairs," or "If we let the girls wear slacks, the next thing you know they'll all be coming in jeans," or "If we don't make them keep their shirttails tucked in, we won't have any discipline." Now they do all come in jeans, shirttails are in or out, the girls wear long dresses, and no one can tell that it's made any difference, except that the children are happier and the teachers have one less rule to try to enforce.

At another elementary school a principal who wanted to go to an extended day proposed the idea to his teachers. They were unenthusiastic. In fact, they came up with all kinds of reasons why it wouldn't work. Finally he said, "Try it for a month. If after that time you don't like it, we will go back to the regular day." They tried it, and they liked it. He made the change he wanted without forcing his faculty to do something they didn't want to do.

Administrators with reluctant faculties need to remind them of the broad purposes of education to keep them from centering on narrow objections, show them what others in the field are doing, bring outside people in to inspire them, and be sure to let them believe that any innovations that result were their ideas in the first place.

◆ MOTIVATING FOR INNOVATING

A classroom teacher knows that to successfully launch a unit of study, she must motivate students if the unit is to be a meaningful learning experience. Motivating techniques may include using pictures and media, questions, field trips, resource people, and student interest. The school principal has the same resources available as the teacher to motivate his faculty for innovation.

When a school in our district changed to a twelve-month plan, it was because there was a need and because the principal had motivated his faculty and community toward this change. The school community had grown rapidly, and the school building wasn't large enough to accommodate all the students. Many children were being bussed to other schools. There were neither plans nor money for a new school, and the faculty and community were troubled and concerned.

The principal arranged for several teachers, parents, and himself to visit other districts around the country that had a twelve-month plan. These people attended conferences and drew up plans for implementing the program in their school. They met with parents and teachers to explain their plan. Their enthusiasm convinced the faculty and the community, and with school board approval, the program began in the fall.

Allowing teachers to feel free to explore ideas without fear of administrative disapproval is another key in motivation. A fine individualized music program in an elementary school evolved because the teacher was allowed to use her talents without administrative interference. In this particular program, children are taught by the teacher to play different instruments such as guitars, drums, organ, and bass viols. (The teacher made two of the bass viols herself.) When a child is not playing an instrument, he is listening to music in individual listening centers.

Teachers had to be motivated before our school joined the Individually Guided Education Program, because it takes a totally committed staff to become officially involved with this organization. Organizationally and philosophically our school was on the way to adopting the IGE concepts, and that was one motivating factor. However, the staff was not aware of IGE as a program for schools.

We arranged for our team leaders to attend a three-day IGE institute planned and conducted by the state department of education. At this institute every detail of IGE was discussed in large and small groups of teachers and administrators. The team leaders saw value in the program, and their reports persuaded the faculty to joint the organization. Motivating the team leaders had in turn motivated the faculty.

A faculty opposed to change may be motivated to try something new that has succeeded elsewhere in the school building. If only one or two teachers want to launch a new program, let them, but if such a request does not come from the teachers, meet with them in small groups to acquaint them with new ideas and to try to move them forward. Innovative programs do not necessarily need to sweep the whole school at the same time—nor should they. Often small pilot programs are best because the unexpected happens on a small scale, and bugs can be worked out before too many students are affected. The staff learns from the experience of other teachers and weighs the value of the program before they become totally committed. Those who weren't enthusiastic in the first place might change their minds when they see a good thing going.

◆ ARRANGING VISITS TO OTHER SCHOOLS

Most teachers enjoy visiting other schools to gain new ideas. It is a chance for a teacher to get away from the routine of everyday activities and to compare his or her teaching activities with those of other teachers. A probable outcome of a school visit is that the teacher-visitor will come back with new ideas.

Like individuals, no two elementary schools are exactly alike and each has certain characteristics that stand out as strengths. Alert teachers will pick up and apply what is good to their own teaching situation.

Visiting for a specific purpose is more helpful than visiting any classroom at random, but how does a teacher know what school has the program he wants to see? If the principal keeps a card file listing schools and the particular strengths of each, the teachers will know where to go. The card file can be kept up to date by having teachers make pertinent comments on the cards when they return from visits. An index is a locater help.

Another way to keep a card index on individual schools is to ask other principals to make out cards for their individual schools at a principals' meeting. These cards can then be duplicated and shared. An example follows:*

NAME OF SCHOOL	DISTRICT
ADDRESS	PHONE
PRINCIPAL	
Teacher contact	
Type of program to visit:	
Teacher contact	
Type of program to visit:	

Add a notation to your card file whenever you hear teachers talking about an exciting program or when you read of one in the paper.

Some superintendents will budget extra funds for school visits, provided the principal and his staff justify the visitation through program improvement. This type of planning should take place six months to a year in advance.

Most superintendents encourage school visits, but in many districts the cost of hiring substitutes to free each teacher for a visit at least once during the school year is prohibitive. Therefore, other ways need to be found to cover classes.

First, explore the "how" with your staff. They are an amazing source of ideas, and they will come up with suggestions such as combining two classes for a short period

* Note: Shared cards should be the same size for filing purposes.

of time to free someone for a visit, suggestions that an administrator would have had little luck imposing upon them. Here are some other possibilities:

◇ Have the special teachers—P.E., music, or librarian—take one or two groups on field trips. They should have volunteer supervisory help.

◇ Dismiss school (in some districts this is possible) for one-half day. The entire staff can then go visiting. Be sure to plan ahead and notify parents well in advance.

◇ Let the principal take over for a teacher, or even two teachers, releasing them for one-half day.

◇ If there are supervisors, counselors, or coordinators on the staff, press them into service. It will be good for them to refresh themselves with a classroom situation.

◆ ALERTING THE STAFF TO NEW PROGRAMS THROUGH IN-SERVICE EDUCATION

Workshops, conferences, and resource people can help prepare a staff for change by giving teachers opportunities to learn of innovations in their field and ways to implement them.

Teachers are not as anxious to attend in-service programs as they are to visit other schools, partly because most of this training takes place after school and at night. Teachers are busy people, and in-service activities take more of their time. If a district dismisses school early for such purposes or offers professional growth credit as an incentive, enthusiasm and attendance pick up. Actually, if in-service is worthwhile, it should take place during school hours when all teachers are present and still have the energy to get something out of it.

Because our superintendent believed that, "A district could change without improving, but could not improve without changing," our district sponsored a drive-in conference on individualized instruction, which was specifically for district teachers but open to other interested educators close enough to drive to it. No fees were charged district teachers, and school was dismissed on Friday so they could attend. The conference itself was innovative in that a school district sponsored it.

District teachers not only attended the conference, they helped put on the program. Teachers brought materials that they actually used in their classrooms for demonstration purposes. Some involved their students in project demonstrations. Teachers freely distributed materials for conference participants to take home, and they wrote summaries that were sent to participants after the conference.

Nationally known people such as William Glasser, author of *Schools Without Failure* (New York: Harper & Row, 1969), were brought in to speak to the group. Thus, those attending were given an overall view of challenges facing the schools as well as learning about specific ways and means to implement new programs. Fees charged participants from outside the district helped defray expenses.

In Denver recently the city's Commission on Community Relations put together a community education workshop. It invited teams of ten people from each of thirty-two schools and communities around the city. A team included a school administrator, two teachers, two parents, and three persons from the school's community.

In the morning the teams toured Denver Public School institutions such as the Diagnostic Teaching Center where individual teaching prescriptions are worked out for children with learning disabilities. In an afternoon session participants discussed programs that couldn't be included on the tour, such as the mountain outdoor education center, in addition to talking over what they had seen in the morning.

This workshop not only gave teachers and administrators a chance to see what their colleagues were doing, but it also exposed laymen from the community to the good going on in their schools.

On a smaller scale, in-service workshops within a school also stimulate change. Gear these workshops to staff needs, and they will be more meaningful. For example, our staff felt a need to improve relationships with each other through freer and more direct communication. Changing attitudes is sometimes necessary before program changes can proceed.

Although the subject of relationships between people isn't innovative, perhaps a workshop on the subject is. A person's human interrelationships are now called his affective domain, so we planned a workshop on affective education. We brought in a college professor who had put on workshops in the area to organize one for the staff in our building. The district gave teachers who attended professional growth credit.

Resource people, such as college professors, book company consultants, and teacher specialists, are sources of help and information when changes are under consideration. The staff should consult with them before major change takes place, because new programs go more smoothly when the staff has had some background information rather than progressing entirely through trial and error.

Before changing the reading program you might plan a workshop or a series of meetings on the subject. For instance, the staff might listen to a college professor discuss theory and methods and a reading specialist discuss books and materials. They might hear what teachers involved in similar reading programs have to say. If, after looking at the proposed change from all sides, the teachers decide to proceed, it will be with more confidence and assurance that the change will be better for the children they teach.

◆ SHARING STAFF KNOWLEDGE AND IDEAS

Principals can't afford to overlook the knowledge and ideas of individual staff members as a factor for change. Free exchange of ideas among the staff encourages even traditional teachers to try something new.

There must be time and opportunity, however, for idea exchanges to occur. A team teaching arrangement seems to provide this and also serves as an incentive for teachers to cooperate rather than compete with each other.

When we began team teaching, we changed our traditional once-a-week faculty meetings to once every three weeks so that grade level and cross-grade level meetings could be held the weeks between. This arrangement gave the staff more opportunity for discussion than did the large group faculty meetings.

As an example of what goes on in grade level meetings, one team of teachers picked a subject, such as math, and exchanged ideas about how each taught certain concepts. They picked a different subject each time they met. They planned their meetings, and they were relevant.

Generally, the faculty were more enthusiastic about grade level and cross-grade level meetings than they were about faculty meetings. Faculty meetings are still important, but they should always be geared toward staff improvement and involvement. If meetings become merely a time when the principal reads a sheet of announcements that could just as well be printed in a bulletin, they might as well be done away with altogether.

One way to share ideas at faculty meetings is to meet each time in a different classroom. Schedule ahead so teachers will know when the group is to meet in their room. The classroom teacher can begin the meeting by taking a few minutes to tell of exciting things the class is doing. The staff meantime observes bulletin boards, classroom projects, or individual pupil projects displayed in the room. Even the furniture arrangement is an idea source, especially for the teacher who is still setting up rows of desks and chairs.

Some faculties have a potpourri once or twice a year. At a potpourri teachers display and demonstrate art, math, social studies, or language arts projects in a carnival atmosphere. Teachers wander from table to table and learn from each other. A project like this takes planning, but it is a social as well as an educational affair. Schedule it for half of a school day, after school, or in conjunction with a pot-luck dinner.

INCLUDING
PARENTS AND COMMUNITY
IN INNOVATION PLANS

"Show and Tell"
❖❖❖❖❖

A SMALL BOY ORDERED A BOWL OF HOT CEREAL IN A restaurant. "Do you like your oatmeal?" his mother asked.

"It's okay," he replied, "but it's not as good as the kind you make. This doesn't have any lumps."

It seems to be human nature to resist change, even change for the better. We like and feel comfortable with what we are used to, and this is as true of parents' and communities' attitudes toward schools as of any other situation.

Parents tend to remember and romanticize the good and to forget the bad about the schools they attended. If they succeeded and were happy, they may see no need for change, or they may think, "What was good enough for me, is good enough for my child." Thus when you propose a change in your school program, you can expect that not all parents will be overjoyed, no matter how convincingly you present your innovations as improvements.

When you set out to make changes, anticipate the negative attitudes that some parents will have about your new programs. Parents have heard stories about innovative schools, and some have had experience with them. One parent told about the open space school his child had attended. "Oh, they taught the three R's all right," he said,

"Running, Roaming, and Raising Hell." Another told of his child spending a six-week grading period in the lavatory. Until grades came out, and he didn't have any, no one knew that he wasn't attending class.

The stories may be exaggerated, but too often a discipline breakdown accompanies a new program. Some educators have mistaken freedom to do whatever one pleases for freedom of choice. Schools can make changes without chaos, but parents have to be convinced.

Preparing parents for change is better than repairing relations after the change has come about. The following example illustrates this point.

The numbers of our fourth and fifth graders had increased during the autumn to the point where it was necessary to add a teacher after Christmas vacation. Creating either a new fourth- or fifth-grade classroom would not solve the problem because it would still leave one grade overcrowded. Teachers involved favored a multi-age classroom, but they knew that many parents do not like combination rooms because they erroneously believe that the top level of one age group is placed with the bottom level of the other. A middle-of-the-year change is always difficult, and in this case many would be affected since children would be moved from seven different homeroom classes to create the eighth classroom.

We began by sending a letter home explaining the situation. The letter read:

> Our enrollment in each of the classrooms for Units D and E, fourth and fifth grades, has increased and now ranges between thirty and thirty-three pupils. We feel that these numbers are too high for effective teaching, especially when we are trying to individualize instruction. Consequently, the administration has decided to reduce the pupil-teacher ratio in each of these classrooms by adding an additional teacher to the faculty.
>
> The staff has discussed several plans for reorganizing Units D and E. Whatever we do, we want to do what is

best for your children. We also feel that the concerns
of parents should be part of our reorganization plan.

We therefore wish to ask you to respond to the following, keeping in mind what you feel is best for your child.

We went on to list alternatives and to ask for parent
opinions on the grouping patterns we offered. In the letter
we described the multi-age group as a combination class for
communication's sake.

When the opinionnaires came back, some parents had
requested the combination class, some did not care or had
no opinion, and some were strongly opposed. Some fifth-
grade parents feared their child would be considered slow
if he were put with fourth graders. One father of a fifth-
grade child called the combination class a "fourth and a half
grade." Another father said, "I don't have any objections to
a combination classroom, but don't move my child."

We organized the class based on parent response and sent
a follow-up letter to inform parents of the staff decision and
the placement of their children. If any parent indicated he
strongly opposed the combination room, his child was not
moved. We missed on two placements, mainly because the
children did not take the letters home and teachers interpreted no response to mean consent; parent conferences
were necessary, but on the whole the change went smoothly
with minor repercussions.

Contrast this with a school that moved students into a
combination situation, then sent a notice home, and had a
delegation of parents in the principal's office the next morning. Maybe the secret is to let parents feel they are participants in, rather than recipients of, a decision.

When an innovation such as year-round school concerns
the entire community, it is best to involve community people
in the planning stage. People resent what is imposed upon
them "for their own good." For instance, school authorities
in a large school system decided that because most students
in a particular high school did not go on to college, they

needed more vocational training. Without consulting anyone from the community, they went ahead and installed
equipment and planned the program. When school opened
in the fall, the school community was "up in arms." The
fact is they might have agreed if they had been consulted
in the first place, but since they hadn't been, they were
opposed.

The Ford Foundation's Comprehensive School Improvement Program is another case in point. The Foundation
poured money into a number of "lighthouse" schools where
they incorporated the newest innovations—open space,
team teaching, flexible scheduling, differentiated staffing,
and technology. The Foundation hoped that these schools
would serve as guides for schools around the country. However, when it came time to evaluate the program, it found
that the innovations were not as long-lasting or as far-
reaching as it had hoped. The reasons were varied, but the
fact that it had not initially involved the parents and the
community in planning and implementing the innovations
was a contributing factor.

There is a dilemma here. If changes are imposed before a
community is ready to accept them, they are not effective;
yet if you wait for the community to be in complete accord
with the changes you plan to make, you probably will not
make any changes at all. So you have to work somewhere
in the middle, giving in where you have to, while effecting
what changes you can as smoothly as possible.

◆ WORKING THROUGH PARENT
   ORGANIZATIONS

Work through your parent organization to win school and
community leaders' support before you attempt a major
school-wide change. If they believe in what you are doing,
they will influence others.

Many schools now have their own parent-teacher organization rather than belonging to the national PTA because

the PTA requires dues and adherence to national rules and regulations. A school's own parent organization can be open to any parent, dues paying or not, and it is freer to meet the needs of the local district.

Most parent organizations operate through an executive board, headed by elected officers and selected committee members. Explain your proposed program to the board first. Then form a joint study committee composed of parents, teachers, and the principal to study the program and report to the board. Once a program has been decided upon, the board can present it to the whole organization.

A parent task force is another vehicle for change. A task force researches a problem and comes up with possible solutions or alternatives to the present situation for the school authorities to consider. It is important to set guidelines so that task force members understand they are a recommending body without authority to make changes on their own.

As an example of minor change, we wanted to improve our school playground. The president of the parent organization appointed a task force. Together they visited other school playgrounds and talked with key members of the community. One woman on the force was also on the city's Greenbelt Planning Committee and had contacts with experts in recreational facility planning. The task force's final plans called for new challenging playground equipment, landscaping, and improved safety conditions for existing facilities. Their plans were practical and educationally sound, and they will be implemented as the budget allows.

Parents working on an individual basis in parent organizations or school-sponsored volunteer programs are good publicity agents for innovative programs. There is an old expression, "A mule can't pull and kick at the same time." No comparison with hard-working volunteers is intended here, but when parents have inside knowledge and working experience with a new program, they usually support it. Their positive attitudes will influence other members of the community, and the results may be more far-reaching than anticipated.

◆ ORIENTATION PROGRAMS

Parent orientation programs are another way to prepare parents for change. It doesn't matter whether parents meet in large or small groups, in school auditoriums, in classrooms, or in individual homes so long as the proposed program change is explained to their satisfaction.

The size of an orientation group can run anywhere from a large percentage of the school's parent population to a small group of ten or fifteen parents. However, some of the most successful parent programs that we have had were basically organized with groups of twenty to twenty-five parents. They were brought together for a group presentation. Then they dispersed to individual centers where overhead projectors, display materials, video tapes, and tape recordings expanded on the proposed program and answered their questions. They had a chance to meet with teachers or the principal on a one-to-one basis and to individually voice their concerns.

You do need to answer parent questions, but it is better to answer them individually or in small group sessions rather than at a large open meeting. For one thing, when questions come from the floor in an auditorium or gymnasium, it is often difficult to hear or be heard. For another, one parent with a negative attitude can needlessly upset the whole group. Finally, if you have a speaker followed by a question and answer period, you hold a captive audience. Those who may not have questions are forced to listen to those who do, and what concerns one parent may not concern others.

When our staff decided to go into the Individually Guided Education Program, we used several methods of parent orientation. First, a principal's newsletter went home with the children. It emphasized the point that IGE fit the school's philosophy and organizational pattern and kept the information on a positive note.

Then during back-to-school night, the principal conducted a large group meeting in the auditorium. He used overhead materials to explain the overall aspects of IGE, such as the organizational pattern, learning program, and in-service activities for teachers.

After the meeting parents moved to the classrooms. The classroom programs varied, depending upon the plans of each team of teachers. We didn't try for standard classroom presentations because individual teachers were better able to understand the concerns of their students' parents and how they could meet them. Most of the teachers used individual display centers and distributed handout materials that included schedules and course content. Preplanning helped account for the success of the orientation.

IGE requires follow-up programs. This is important because new parents move into the school district and because parents tend to forget and to misconstrue ideas.

Coffee klatches held at school or in private homes and sponsored by the parent organization provide an opportunity to orient newcomers. These get-togethers not only give the principal a chance to talk about the school's instructional program, but they also make newcomers feel welcome and help them meet the people of the community.

For an ever-ready orientation program, set up a parent learning center in the school library. Collect and make available materials that tell about the school, its programs, and policies. Put out pamphlets available at low cost from various publishing companies for general parent information. Display materials that will help parents understand new programs. A library filmstrip projector or tape recorder can be stored in the center, so you won't need to buy new equipment if you want to use filmstrips and tapes.

An orientation center lets you meet parents' needs on an individual basis.

◆ COMMUNICATION TECHNIQUES

No matter how well you plan for and prepare orientation programs, it is to no avail if parents don't attend. If a parent tells you that he or she heard about the meeting or a new program by word of mouth from a neighbor and you have sent notices or newsletters home, you know that something is wrong, either with your message or your messengers.

One way to remind students to deliver a message is to have each teacher stamp students' hands with a stamp that says, "Message Coming Home" or "Meeting Tonight." Use the kind of ink grocery stores use to stamp their meat "Choice" or whatever. The ink is harmless and washes right off. Students, especially primary children, love to be stamped, and if they still forget to mention that they have a message, a parent usually asks, "What's that on your hand?" and then they remember.

A parent telephone committee is another way to send out a message. Two or three volunteers call the homeroom mothers, then the homeroom mother calls five other parents from an assigned list. These five parents contact another five, or however it works out, until all parents are contacted.

One problem with this method, though, is that it is like the old game of gossip where each person whispers a message to the next person. By the time the message reaches the last person, it isn't the original message. Try to be sure that each person understands the message. Asking each person who calls a group to repeat the message will help avoid misunderstanding.

Assuming a written message arrives home, the following guidelines may help you put it across:

◇   Clarity is most important. Say what you have to say simply. Avoid using difficult words, long sentences, abstract ideas, and words that only educators use. Most parents would not understand an expression such as "cognitive domain."

◇   Think about what your parents need to know. The question you need to answer as you write is, "How does it affect me and my child?"

◇   Make key points visible by underlining and use of italics and capital letters.

◇   Make every word count.

◇   Make the message as personal as possible.

◇   Repeat and summarize thoughtfully.

Since the principal is most often the one who initially presents a new program to parent audiences, what he says and the way he says it may determine parents' attitudes toward the program. The following guidelines apply to oral messages:

◇   Avoid educational jargon and use mostly one, two, or three syllable words.

◇   Express your ideas to your audience and don't try to impress them with vague ideas.

◇   Use factual information and avoid misuse of facts.

◇   Keep your presentation loose in style. It should sound spontaneous rather than rehearsed and memorized.

◇   Reinforce points through repetition.

Educational jargon is probably the biggest communication barrier between educators and others. Educators toss around words formed by the initial letters of professional organizations or terms that could mean two different things, such as non-graded (this one even confuses educators), or terms like behavioral objectives, which if taken literally seems to mean deportment.

It is no wonder parents are confused. They are bombarded by terms. They may not know what you are talking about, but they won't ask for fear of appearing stupid. So say it in plain English is the best advice, whether you are writing or talking to a parent or community group.

Since communications are two way, how you listen is as important as how you write or speak. If parents know you want to hear what they say and that you will consider their ideas seriously, they are more likely to be candid and to tell you what's bothering them. If, on the other hand, you view parents as a threat and wish they would stay away, they might, but they will talk with other parents. A new program will not succeed when parents are muttering against it.

Unfortunately, there are people who enjoy starting rumors, and new programs are grist for their mill. If you feel it is necessary, have a rumor control center run by the parent organization or yourself, where parents can call to check out rumors.

Keep the lines of communication open, and you will minimize problems. But it is one thing to say, "Yes, we need and expect good communication with our parents," and another thing to follow through and see to it that communication channels stay open.

INDIVIDUALIZING FOR LEARNING

"Every Child a Winner"
❖❖❖❖❖

A MOTHER WHO PACKED A CAN OF SODA OR PUDDING WITH A pull-tab top in her son's lunch always put a Band-Aid in the sack because she knew that he might cut his finger. She was doing for her son what modern schools are trying to do for all of their students—individualizing.

Years ago educators talked about individual differences, but there didn't seem to be specific plans for how to provide for them. Today the phrase is "individualizing instruction," and schools are implementing new programs to put individualization into effect.

◆ WHAT IS INDIVIDUALIZING INSTRUCTION?

Individualizing instruction means different things to different people, educators as well as parents. Some think it means that each child in the room is doing his own thing. Some think it means instruction on a one-to-one basis. Some think it is each child going through worksheets or packets at his own rate. Some believe it is grouping children according to their needs.

We believe it is providing an opportunity for each child to work at a level where he finds interest and success. He might do this in a group situation or working by himself, and he might do it in a traditional as well as in an open space building.

Individualizing is tuning in on the student and trying to meet his needs. For example, a tall mature boy in one school complained that the school lunch was not enough to satisfy his hunger. He asked if he could buy adult lunch tickets. Foreseeing bookkeeping complications that might arise when other students wanted to buy adult lunch tickets because of the prestige involved, the principal talked to the cook. She suggested that this boy remind her that he was David as he went through the lunch line, and she would see that he had enough. Now, when she sees David coming, she heaps his plate high.

Individualizing is respect for and recognition of the child as an individual. Students don't want to be known as black or white, upper-middle class or disadvantaged, Catholic or Protestant—they want to be known as the individuals they are. In some of the big modern high schools, students are identified by their IBM numbers. If they are absent, their numbers instead of their names are sent to the attendance office. This may be more efficient, but it does take the humanism out of the school. We believe, at least at the elementary level, that students need to be known and identified as individuals.

Children seem pleased and surprised when the principal calls them by name, and even in a large school, it is possible to know all of them. A new principal can start with the kindergartners. If he makes it a point to know the kindergartners, new students, and some others each year, in a few years he will know them all. One principal we know spends ten or fifteen minutes a day reading to the first graders. He feels this has two benefits: first he gets to know their names, and second, they get to know him and come to realize that reading is important to him.

Another principal tells new teachers they won't have as many discipline problems if they stand at their doors and greet students by name as they enter the rooms. His theory has not been substantiated by any study of which we know, but an individual greeting may make some difference in behavior.

Individual identification, however, is only a small part of the total concept. A visitor doesn't have to be told whether or not a school is committed to individualization. Individualization is reflected throughout the building. There is tangible evidence from a sign in the faculty lounge that reads "Every Child A Winner" to the creative learning centers in the classrooms, to the student art, writing, science, and social studies projects proudly displayed in the halls. There is intangible evidence in the quick friendly smiles and warm "Hellos" a visitor receives as he walks down the halls or into the classrooms and observes children who seem to be enjoying what they are doing.

◆ FITTING THE PROGRAM TO THE CHILD THROUGH CONTINUOUS PROGRESS IN THE OPEN CLASSROOM

Hopefully there aren't any teachers still trying to teach left-handed children to write with their right hands. This was one of many ways teachers used to try to teach children to adapt to the school, regardless of the effect on the child. Instead of changing children to fit the school, schools need to change to fit the children they are serving.

One way to better serve the child and provide for his individual differences is to initiate a continuous progress or non-graded program in an open classroom. We use the term continuous progress because it isn't as confusing or upsetting to parents as the term non-graded. Some parents think non-graded means the school has done away with grades such as As or Bs, while others think it means the children are put in a classroom with children of all ages.

Continuous progress simply means that the school reduces the range of subject matter to be taught by breaking the curriculum into small, logical, sequential steps through which the child progresses at his own rate. Although this sounds as if all the children are programmed to do the same thing, they have alternatives through choices of methods and materials at each step.

Learning objectives are established and clearly understood by students and teacher. An oral or written pretest and post-test before and after the student has used multimedia materials determine whether or not the student has met his objectives. Of course, there are check points along the way, too, so a child does not get too far off the track before he receives help, but this is essentially the way the program works.

There are many advantages in continuous progress. Two are that since children progress through learning steps at their own rate, no child is asked to repeat what he has already learned, and there is always a challenge ahead for an eager learner. Meanwhile, the slower learner isn't continually frustrated by trying to keep up. If children are ready to use materials usually reserved for the next grade, they may, and if they need to use materials below their grade level, they may do this too.

Continuous progress also provides for placing children who have been absent for a long period of time and makes it easier to place children who have entered from another school district.

Another point in its favor is that it enables the teacher to use a wide variety of materials in the classroom at little or no additional cost. Since these schools no longer need to order sets of thirty to thirty-five books per class, because students busy at different learning tasks don't use the same book at the same time, several different sets may be purchased and divided among the classrooms. In addition, many publishers are breaking down their materials so schools may purchase just the sections or chapters they want. The variety of learning materials increases alternatives and furthers the goal of individualization.

Teachers agree, with hardly an exception, that children

are different, and this fact must constantly be considered; but when it comes to initiating a continuous progress program, some teachers will oppose it because of the additional work involved. As in most other programs, success or failure depends on staff implementation, so committing the staff is the first step toward continuous progress.

Once the staff is committed, you may wonder how to start. *Start with one subject.* A school does not have to go into a total program all at once. Our program started with reading and evolved slowly over a period of years. Because it was slow, the transition was smooth; but with the number of commercial programs now available, schools wishing to start a program out to be able to move considerably faster than we did.

Some schools start continuous progress in math, reading, and language arts. They add social studies and science later when the rest of the program is going smoothly. Meantime, students in a classroom study the same science and social studies units, but individualization takes place through choices of projects and materials. When teachers feel comfortable with one or two subjects, they will move ahead with others. This is better than trying too much at once and giving up in despair when the program doesn't work.

Continuous progress has to be school-wide or a move from one teacher to another the next year causes problems because a child who has moved ahead has nowhere to go. However, teachers should be allowed to begin their programs in their own way. One teacher started her class at the beginning of the year as she always had, in one big group. When she felt she was ready, she started one student in an individualized reading program. When he was going along well at his own pace, she asked him to start someone else, and so on until the entire class was started. She only had to show one student. Other teachers begin by dividing the class in half and starting half the class at a time. Still others start with a group of five or six. Whatever works for a particular teacher is right.

One question that parents ask is what will happen if they move to a school that doesn't have continuous progress. We answer that by telling them that we send students' reading and math levels on to the next school and it will be up to that school to place them on levels where they belong. The same is true of the junior high school. We work closely with the junior high in our area, and it places our students according to the levels they have achieved. However, if you do not have a good relationship with your junior high, and it makes no provision for differentiating its teaching, then you will have to go ahead and send the students on as you have prepared them. Student and parent protest might bring about changes there, but you can't wait to improve your program until the junior high is ready.

Continuous progress activities go on in open classrooms, but the open classroom is not synonomous with open space. Open classroom is a concept whereby the student is free to pursue his objectives at his individual pace.

The following stories illustrate the difference between the open and closed concept in the classroom. Both incidents took place in a conventional building.

A new principal walked into a classroom. The children sat at desks in straight rows. The teacher was talking; the students were quiet. The teacher, probably because she was nervous at the principal's visit, wrote $17 + 5 = 12$ on the blackboard. Not a child in the room moved or snickered. Walls not only surrounded the room, they were almost visible between teacher and students.

In another school the principal walked into a classroom and had to look for a few minutes before he could find the teacher. She was in a corner with a group of children. There were at least five different groups doing five different things, while some students were working independently. There was a hum of activity. The principal went over to the teacher and handed her her paycheck. One of the boys looked up. "What is that?" he asked. "Her paycheck," the principal answered. The boy seemed surprised. "Where does she work?" he asked. In this case the classroom walls were not limiting.

Actually, it only appeared that the teacher was not working. Individualizing in an open classroom is a demanding way to teach. The teacher must plan and organize or the program will not succeed, but in the process he becomes a guide and a consultant, a facilitator of learning, rather than an authority figure who gives orders. For example, a little girl brought home a particularly good picture from her open classroom. The mother commented, "That's good. Did your teacher like it?" The little girl looked at her with a bewildered who-the-heck-cares look and said, "Why?"

An open learning atmosphere such as this does not pit students against teacher. Since there is no contest, students direct their energies toward learning rather than continually trying to test the teacher.

There are many activities going on at the same time in an open classroom, and the teacher cannot be everywhere at once. Therefore, students need to make their own decisions, run their own machines, learn to use the resource centers to advantage, check their own work, and keep many of their own records. They have to take responsibility, so they become more independent learners, and they learn how to learn as they acquire skills. They have to become involved. They can no longer tune out and do nothing while the teacher talks or other students answer questions. In an open, continuous progress program the student soon realizes that unless he participates, nothing happens. His learning depends on what he does, not on what the teacher does for him.

◆ GROUPING AND REGROUPING

A small boy asked his mother why his father always brought his briefcase home from the office. His mother explained that it was because his father had so much work to do that he couldn't finish all of it at the office. The boy thought for a moment, then he asked, "Why don't they just put him in a slower group?"

Regardless of how adults try to justify ability grouping as best for a child because he can work at his level, when there are high, average, and low classrooms in a school, children are very conscious of their place in the ranking. Continuous progress calls for numerous groups and flexibility in moving from level to level, so a placement does not carry the stigma of ability grouping.

One grouping method for school-wide continuous progress is to assign students in a grade to a specific homeroom teacher according to pupil assessment slips filled out in the spring of the year. Ours ask for reading and math levels and pertinent comments, such as who does not get along with whom, who enjoys being with whom, or who responds well to a male teacher or a strong personality.

At our school each team of teachers sits down together in the spring to work out class assignments. First they divide the students according to reading levels, which in a sixth-grade class might range from fourth-grade second semester to seventh-grade first semester, so that all teachers have students of high, average, and low reading ability. This assures a heterogeneous mixture in every classroom. Then, the teachers make some trades so students who need to be together are together and students who need to be apart are separated. The principal may make some changes too, because he may know of parental biases and previous parent-teacher conflicts involving other family members. It is better to avoid a problem than to be forced to make changes later in the year.

Once the classes are assigned, the teachers on the team regroup for reading. If each of four teachers starts with three reading levels, and the team regroups, there are twelve grouping possibilities. If they regroup again for math after looking at the math levels on the assessment slips, twelve different groups will be created.

Putting two grades together into a multi-age or combination classroom widens the span and increases grouping possibilities. When we organize a multi-age group, we do not look for the high level of one grade and the low level of the other. We look for children who will work well together and whom teachers have recommended as being self-motivated and independent learners.

You may wonder why, if the children are progressing individually at their own rate, it is necessary to group at all. There are times, especially for math and reading, when the teacher needs to teach a concept. It is more efficient to teach it to a group than to repeat it five or six times. It is also essential to vary activities or children become bored. They do not want to learn by themselves all day any more than they want to be teacher directed for a long period of time.

Finally, some children need to work with a group as much as some children need to work alone. Providing them with that opportunity is individualizing instruction for them. Teachers, therefore, group for efficiency, variety, and to individualize instruction.

◆ MAKING REPORT FORMS RELEVANT

If a child is encouraged to work through learning steps at his own rate, then why should he be compared to the rest of the class by a letter grade? What teacher hasn't agonized over a child who has worked hard to make progress but is still doing D work when compared to others?

It is almost unheard of for a student to fail P.E. if he puts on his gym suit and attends class. He isn't made to feel like a failure because he can't throw a ball as far or run as fast as someone else. This is understandable, because we realize that some students are more coordinated than others. Yet a student who has trouble with reading or math is compared unfavorably by grades with others his age. Sometimes, even if he always "puts on his gym suit" and comes to class, he fails.

Those who argue against grades contend that parents who

feel their self-image is tied to their childrens' grades exert pressure that ranges to payment for or punishment for not getting good grades. This in turn causes some children to resort to cheating. Grades have become the end, students are marked, identified, and pigeonholed for life by the grades they make in school.

Most educators would do away with grades altogether if it were not for parental pressure. In many communities parents, especially parents of students who earn As and Bs, still want to see how their children rank in relation to others and are not yet satisfied with a progress report. They argue that grades are an incentive for excellence.

Judging by the variety of report forms we see when we enroll new students from all over the country, educators are searching for a way to effectively communicate a child's progress to parents without damaging his self-concept. Some schools are compromising and giving a letter grade when parents insist upon it and a report of progress when they do not.

Use of the child's performance as criteria for evaluation is increasing. Where report cards used to state a subject area followed by a letter grade, there are now statements more descriptive of pupil behavior. An example of a section of a report form in mathematics may state:

—Knows arithmetic facts
    —addition   —subtraction
    —multiplication   —division
—Shows satisfactory speed and accuracy in computation
—Understands basic concepts that have been presented
—Solves problems correctly
—Solves problems consistently
—Uses reasoning in solving problems

A parent-student-teacher conference, together with a report form noting skills the child has mastered or areas where he is experiencing difficulties, is individual and relevant reporting. The child is included because it is better to talk with him than about him. If he helps establish his goals and participates in evaluating his achievements, he can see whether or not he has made progress.

Some schools complain that parents don't come to conferences, so conference reporting isn't effective. One school handles this problem by telling parents they must come to the conference if they want a report. No reports are mailed or sent home. This is a bold move, but the school reports over a ninety per cent response.

A school in Nashville, Tennessee, uses a simple form. It tells parents their child is doing well in _____. The staff thinks he can do better in _____. You can help by _____.

Another school notes the date a child enters and leaves each math and reading level and where he stands at conference time.

Continuous reporting is as important as continuous progress. Parents like to know what's going on. One parent, who was told at conference time that her son hadn't done much during the reporting period, bitterly complained that during the intervening time no one had called to tell her, "The little fink was goofing off."

On the positive side, a school in Indiana sends home a promotion report every time a child enters a new reading level. They individualize their reports too, with printed "he" and "she" letters.

Because teachers are so directly involved, they should participate in making up a report form relevant to their school. A faculty committee annually evaluates our report form. They consider parent and teacher input and try to come up with something for the following year that is an improvement over what we have been using. Right now we are using a report form that the teachers fill out beforehand to go over with parents at conference time.

Our guidelines for developing written evaluation forms for reporting pupil progress and a copy of our current report forms follow, not because we think our report forms are ideal—they aren't, and not because everyone at our school is satisfied with them—but because we hope that between the guidelines and the report forms, you might find some ideas that can be adapted to develop a meaningful form for your school.

GREENWOOD SCHOOL
GUIDELINES FOR DEVELOPING WRITTEN EVALUATION FORMS FOR REPORTING PUPIL PROGRESS

◇ Follow school philosophy, i.e., show continuous progress through the school program, individualize as much as possible.

◇ Statements written in behavioral terms, i.e., evaluate on an observable and measurable basis rather than subjective, and avoid making value judgments.

◇ Provide for parent feedback.

◇ Make report form as easy as possible to fill out.

◇ System should report progress in all areas of growth—physical, mental, social, emotional.

◇ Evaluation should be basic to curriculum improvement.

◇ Evaluation should be based on comprehension of the abilities and needs of each child as a growing individual instead of being based on a comparison of one child to another.

◇ All concerned should participate; the child being evaluated should have a share in determining objectives, selecting techniques of appraisal, and interpreting results.

◇ Evaluation should be descriptive in terms of desired behavior.

◇ Evaluation should be good for the child whose behavior is being appraised—procedures should be *fair, positive* and *nondestructive* in their total effect. The child should be permitted to keep his self-respect.

GREENWOOD ELEMENTARY SCHOOL
CHERRY CREEK SCHOOL DISTRICT
PUPIL PROGRESS REPORT

NAME _____ UNIT _____ TEACHER _____

QUARTER _____ _____ SCHOOL YEAR _____

SUBJECT	LEVEL	ACHIEVE-MENT	EFFORT	LEVEL	ACHIEVE-MENT	EFFORT	COMMENTS
READING							
Comprehension							
Skills							
Vocabulary							
LANGUAGE							
Expresses ideas clearly: a. Written							
b. Oral							
Grammar Usage: a. Written							
b. Oral							
SPELLING							
Required list							
Written work							
PENMANSHIP							
ARITHMETIC							
Knows basic facts with speed and accuracy							
Knows four basic operations of arithmetic							
Uses reasoning ability							
SOCIAL STUDIES							
Shows an understanding of our/other cultures							
Applies reference skills in reporting							
Contributes to projects and discussions							
SCIENCE							
Shows an inquiring mind							
Contributes to projects and discussions							
ART							

PERMANENT RECORD

GREENWOOD ELEMENTARY SCHOOL
CHERRY CREEK SCHOOL DISTRICT
PUPIL PROGRESS REPORT

NAME _____

QUARTER ___ ___

ATTITUDES AND PRACTICES AFFECTING PROGRESS			COMMENTS
Shows self-discipline			
Has developed good listening skills			
Follows directions			
Works independently			
Completes work in allowed time			
Shows initiative			

KEY: H - High quality
          S - Satisfactory
          N - Needs improvement
        NA - Not applicable
       ___ - Satisfactory
        _x_ - Needs improvement

LEVELS: I - Most difficult
          II -
          III -
          IV -
          V - Least difficult

Assignment for school year 19_____, 19_____

TEACHER _____

PRINCIPAL _____

PERMANENT RECORD

INDIVIDUALIZING
THE CURRICULUM

"Adapting Materials Is Better Than Adopting Texts"
❖❖❖❖

IT USED TO BE THAT WHEN SCHOOL OPENED IN THE FALL, teachers, short a few books for the number of children in their classrooms, rushed into the principal's office to see if they couldn't get more—fast!

If a teacher did this today, we would be concerned about what was going on in his room. Whatever it was, it wouldn't be individualization, because a teacher who is individualizing would never need a full set of books. He would be using multi-media, multi-level material to fashion an individualized curriculum.

Fashioning an individualized curriculum for a child is like ordering a custom-made suit of clothing. First, measurements are taken; then, with a wearing objective in mind, material is selected, and at a final fitting, the finished product is evaluated.

The same four steps apply to individualizing the curriculum, otherwise "the suit may not do." The steps in educational terms are: preassessment of the child's needs, setting realistic learning objectives, providing the teaching program, and evaluation. This process is often called a learning cycle, since, theoretically, it is ongoing and continuous. Good teachers have been using the cycle for years, whether or not they recognize it as such, so it is not really new, just recently identified.

Because an understanding of the four steps is essential to any curriculum study, further explanations follow:

1. *Preassessment of the child's needs.* Simple logic tells us that we need to know what the child knows before he attempts something. For example, a teacher might be about to teach division of whole numbers. If a child is proficient at this, he would be wasting his time doing division. If another child can't multiply numbers, he would be lost. Identifying what children know through commercial tests, teacher tests, or other means, therefore, becomes important.

2. *Setting realistic learning objectives.* Once a child's needs are identified, the teacher must set (this may be cooperative between child and teacher) the objectives he should meet related to the lesson. These goals need not be long and complicated, but rather ones that can be observed and measured as the child pursues the learning task. In the case of fractions and decimals, an objective might be to write fractions in decimal form.

3. *Providing the teaching program.* Here the teacher has latitude in helping the child. He helps the child select media that he is to use, such as books, filmstrips, and tapes; he groups the child, either with others who have similar objectives or by himself for independent study; finally he decides, if someone is to work with the child, who that someone will be—an aide, another child, a parent volunteer, a student teacher, or the teacher himself. Many call this managing the teaching-learning program.

4. *Evaluation or assessment.* Assuming proper checks have been made along the way, a child will have successfully completed the objective he set out to learn. Assessment may be written or oral, and it may be the start of the next learning objective.

Individualizing the curriculum does not mean what some

newer schools have taken it to mean, i.e., letting elementary students choose their own curriculum. Some of the new schools have gone overboard in an effort to make the curriculum relevant and have let the students come up with subjects they would like to study, like Swahili, pool, or macramé, while the staff stood by hoping students would pick up some of the basics as they went along.

This isn't to say that cultural and leisure time activities don't have a place in the school program. They can be worked into an extended day schedule, social studies or science units, or a Friday afternoon activity period, but they shouldn't replace basic subjects. If we are preparing students for life, they will need to know how to read, write, spell, and do basic arithmetic.

The three Rs are relevant to all students, so individualization takes place, not through student choice of basic subjects, but in the way one adapts what they all need to learn to the individual learner. Reading, for example, involves more than reading from a book. During a reading class children work with phonics, reading workbooks, and dittos; they do group and individual reading, take part in plays and creative dramatics, and use a reading kit as well as listen to tapes for literature and comprehension.

◆ SELECTING COMMERCIAL MATERIALS

Publishers of commercial materials have recognized the need for an individualized curriculum and have created laboratories or kits to meet the need. The companies have broken the curriculum into small steps, and when you buy their products, you obtain learning or behavioral objectives, pre-tests, learning materials, check tests, and post-tests. In addition, you receive an index to other basic textbooks, giving the page numbers where material relating to a given step can be found.

The kits are expensive, but they serve as a guide, and you can hardly go into an individualized program without them. You can cut costs, buying different kits for different classrooms and letting teachers trade among themselves.

One of the major differences between the new materials and earlier programmed instruction is that in the latter all the necessary material students used was in one package that they went through one step at a time, while the new materials encourage students to use outside sources to complete their objectives. Textbooks, teacher-made materials, reference books, filmstrips, and tapes are all used to supplement the kits. Programmed instruction bored students because they worked with the same sort of materials day after day, but the new curriculum materials offer media variety that the old ones lacked.

This multi-media approach presents a problem for schools in certain states which are limited by state adopted text or texts. The only answer for them until this ceases to be policy seems to be to use as much supplementary material as the law allows.

A wealth of free help and resources concerning curriculum materials are available through the consultant services offered by book publishers. The educational media experts, most of them former teachers, eagerly seek ways to help a faculty implement all or part of their products.

For example, a publisher's representative visited our school recently. He told us of the new things his company was doing and showed us specifically how his materials would help us further individualize our program. In addition, he spent some time with the math chairman discussing grouping patterns and the scope and sequence of math skills. Staff members available when the representative was in the building were eager to hear what he had to say, and in-service training on a small scale took place.

Of course, you can't spend this much time with all book salesmen, but by selecting representatives who seem to be offering materials that fit your needs and by listening to what they have to say, you pick up ideas on how to improve your program. When the time comes to purchase, the principal and a faculty curriculum committee decide together which curriculum materials to keep and which to replace, picking and choosing materials from different companies for a balanced and individualized curriculum.

If you aren't autonomous and have to live with the district's curriculum decisions, it will be more difficult to individualize because what is good for one school in a district may not be good for another. Materials that have to satisfy all the schools end up satisfying none of them. Work toward autonomy through the superintendent and the board, for while centralized purchasing may save some money, it does not compensate for the loss of opportunity to individualize.

Some schools have tried to do on their own what the publishing companies have already done for them. In some cases they didn't know that commercial material, such as the text indexes, were available. In other cases they felt commercial materials were expensive or that they simply wanted to develop their own.

Curriculum work does take time, and at the rate of teacher pay per hour, it is probably far more expensive than outright purchase. Besides the time and the expense, teachers have neither the resources nor the supporting research to come up with curriculum as educationally sound as that which can be purchased. The Ford Foundation, in fact, concluded in *A Foundation Goes to School*, a report concerning its Comprehensive School Improvement Program, that "In terms of both cost and student-teacher learning, the adoption of professionally developed curricula produced far more substantive change than in-house curriculum development."

♦ TEACHER-MADE AND SUPPLEMENTARY MATERIALS

We have been talking about major curriculum design, not about supplementary teacher-made and teacher-provided materials that lend interest and variety to the program. Sometimes an index to basic texts lists nothing available in a particular area except the material provided by the publisher. In this case teachers may want to supplement with their own materials.

Some examples of and suggestions for teacher-made and supplementary materials are:

◇ Slit the spines of old texts that would ordinarily be thrown out and divide what is still good and useful into units for the resource center.

◇ Take sample books sent by book publishers out of the bookroom or off office shelves and put them in the media centers.

◇ Use the encyclopedia as a math supplementary source. While math books assume the student knows something about the subject to begin with, encyclopedias explain a concept from scratch.

◇ Bring in catalogs of all kinds for index and math projects.

◇ Use newspaper ads for math lessons.

◇ Use road maps for geography or math.

◇ Cut up the Sunday comics and mount on cards for sequence study.

◇ Make a measuring device by mounting a wheel on a stick so that every rotation marks a certain distance.

◇ Put out toys, puzzles, and games with simplified teacher-made directions the children can follow without additional help.

When preparing teaching materials, learning centers, and games, it is important to keep these four points in mind:

1. *Self-directive.* The child should be able to read and follow the directions given.

2. *Starter words.* Words such as "do," "read," "write," "try this," "could you," "can you," "something for you," help the child get started.

3. *Attractive.* It should be neat, captivating, illustrative, and offer a task that can be completed in a reasonable amount of time.

4. *Self-corrective.* The child should be able to discover where or how he made an error. He should be able to do it over again correctly should he make mistakes.

♦ INDIVIDUALIZING THE SPELLING PROGRAM

Spelling is one of the easiest subjects in which to implement the basic concepts of individualization. If you want to introduce individualization in your school and don't know where to start, start with spelling.

At a time when there was nothing available from commercial companies, a faculty curriculum committee in our district developed an individualized spelling program. It has been and still is a workable way to teach spelling. It requires basic word lists, based on the most common words children need and can learn at each level. There are many lists from which to choose, among them the Dolch word list—not all-inclusive but a good basic list for a primary spelling program—so teachers don't have to make up their own lists, although they may want to add a few words to take care of unique differences. The key to individualizing spelling is letting children develop individual lists of words they do not know how to spell and then helping them learn to spell those words.

The schedule for a primary child's weekly spelling program in our school follows:

SCHEDULE FOR THE TEACHING OF SPELLING
Grade 2

FIRST DAY

1. Pretest on the basic spelling list.

2. The pretest is checked.

3. Teacher and pupils pronounce basic and supplementary word lists.

4. Pupil is given a duplicate copy of the weekly basic and supplementary word list. He indicates incorrect words on the basic list and then chooses words from the supplementary list to replace the words he spelled correctly. (See sample following the schedule.)

5. Pupil writes his individual spelling list on the bottom of the duplicated sheets. Teacher must recheck each sheet.

6. Teacher files one duplicate sheet for class use, and child retains the second duplicated sheet for further study.

SECOND DAY

1. Teacher groups pupils using information from the pretest.

2. Pupils study individualized lists using these study steps:
   a. Look at the word and say the word.
   b. Say the letters in the word softly.
   c. Cover the word and write it.
   d. Look to see if you spelled the word correctly.
   e. If you made a mistake, cross out the word. *Do not erase.* Go back to step a.

3. Teacher presents words in context for development of meaning.

4. Pupils write spelling words under teacher's supervision emphasizing:
   a. Correct letter formation.
   b. Correct spacing.
   c. Corrections made with a straight line through the incorrect word.
   d. No erasures.

THIRD DAY

1. Time should be provided for study to meet individual spelling needs.

2. Teach the phonetic elements of the spelling words.

3. Teacher dictates sentences to be written. (Maximum of five sentences is recommended.)

4. Pupils proofread sentences.

FOURTH DAY

1. Pupils take final test. (No erasures. One correction is allowed by marking through the word with a straight line.)

2. Teacher checks all papers.

3. Pupil writes the misspelled words correctly to be used in fifth-day exercises.

4. Teacher collects papers and records grades.

FIFTH DAY

Combine language, handwriting, and spelling periods.

1. Group I: The pupils who have missed words on a final test work with teacher, as individuals and in small groups, doing remedial activities. When a pupil's remedial work is finished, he begins the creative writing activity as suggested for Group II.

2. Group II: The pupils with a perfect score on the final test are assigned creative writing activities.
   a. Write original stories, riddles, or poems using words from the spelling lists.
   b. Pupils proofread their written work.

SAMPLE OF DUPLICATED SPELLING LIST
(Make two for each pupil)

NAME _____

DATE _____

Basic	*Supplementary*
read	leaf
road	east
pie	tail
pail	coal
eat	Monday
coat	drop

MY INDIVIDUAL SPELLING LIST

1. _____
2. _____
3. _____
4. _____
5. _____
6. _____

THREE-DAY PLAN FOR PRIMARY REVIEW LESSONS
FOR A SHORTENED WEEK

FIRST DAY

Pretest; teacher selects a maximum of twenty words from the previous basic lists to use for the review test. Teacher checks papers. Pupil makes two copies on duplicated sheets.

SECOND DAY

Use fifth-day plans to provide for individual needs of pupils as indicated by the review test.

THIRD DAY

Final test and correction.

For intermediate children the weekly plan is similar to the primary one but allows for more individual and student-to-student teaching. We call it working with partners because two students exchange their individual word lists.

A weekly plan for an intermediate child follows:

SCHEDULE FOR THE TEACHING OF SPELLING
Grade 4

FIRST DAY

1. Pretest on the basic spelling list.

2. The pretest is checked. (Pupils can do this with teacher supervision.) Pupils record scores.

3. Teacher and pupils pronounce basic and supplementary lists.

4. Pupil prepares his list of words for the week. He indicates the words he has missed and the supplementary words he will use on the duplicated copies of the weekly word list.

5. Pupil writes his individual list on one duplicated sheet and gives it to the teacher for checking.

6. The teacher records scores and files one copy of each child's word list for class use. The pupil retains the other for further study.

SECOND DAY

1. Teacher presents selected words in context for meaning.

2. Teacher presents skill exercises.
    a. Exercises to extend word meanings.
    b. Exercises to clarify word structure.
    c. Exercises to illustrate spelling patterns.
    d. Exercises to strengthen dictionary use.

3. Pupils study individualized lists with teacher supervision using these study steps:
    a. Look at the word and say the word.
    b. Say the letters in the word softly by syllables.
    c. Cover the word and write it.
    d. Look to see if the word is spelled correctly.
    e. If the word is wrong, cross out the word.
       Do not erase. Go back to step a.
       Note: To check spelling, the child *writes* the word. He does not merely spell it aloud.

THIRD DAY

1. Pupils study with partners and/or in small groups to meet individual spelling needs.

2. Pupils work with teacher to apply skills studied on the second day to their own lists of words.

3. Teacher dictates sentences containing spelling words. (Maximum of five sentences is recommended).

FOURTH DAY

1. Pupils take final test. (No erasures. One correction is allowed by marking a straight line through the word.)
    a. Partners administer the test.
    b. Ballpoint pen is used after the second semester of the fourth grade.
    c. Lists are proofread.

2. Partners check test and record final test scores.

FIFTH DAY

1. Pupils record scores from the final test and correct mis-spelled words in their test books.

2. Pupils who have missed words on the final test work with the teacher individually or in small groups doing remedial work. When they are finished they do activities suggested in step 3.

3. Pupils who have perfect scores are assigned activities to enrich the spelling program.
    a. Writing activities.
    b. Proofreading activities.
        Note: Specifice lessons in proofreading for spelling should be taught at the beginning of the year and reviewed periodically.

SAMPLE OF DUPLICATED SPELLING LIST
(Make two for each pupil)

NAME_____

DATE_____

Basic	Supplementary	Individual
choose	title	1._____
present	gases	2._____
laugh	report	3._____
noose	balloon	4._____
thought	distance	5._____
plate	machines	6._____
chose	wheel	7._____
eight	space	8._____
though	hemisphere	9._____
save	pledge	10._____
nose	stratosphere	11._____
outside	product	12._____
through	vapor	13._____
round	beach	14._____
safe	globe	15._____
take	soar	16._____

PLANS FOR REVIEW LESSONS

PLAN 1

FIRST DAY

1. Pretest on a list of words (maximum of thirty) the teacher has selected from the basic lists that have been given.

2. Partners check the tests and record the scores.

SECOND DAY

1. Pupils prepare individual study lists by checking the words missed on two duplicated word lists.

2. Pupil study based on individual needs. (See weekly fifth-day plan.)

THIRD DAY

1. Final test administered by partners.

2. Partners correct papers and record final scores.

PLAN 2

FIRST DAY

1. Pupils choose a maximum of thirty words missed from their partner's test book and test their partner.

2. Partners check tests and record the scores.

SECOND DAY

1. Pupils correct the misspelled words on their test papers and make an additional copy of their word lists for the teacher.

2. Pupil study as based on individual needs. (See weekly fifth-day plan.)

THIRD DAY

1. Final test administered by partners.

2. Partners correct test papers and record scores.

◆ WAYS TO INDIVIDUALIZE CREATIVE WRITING, MUSIC, AND PHYSICAL EDUCATION

Creative writing seems as if it would be individual to begin with, but some teachers take away all the creativity and individuality by assigning the same dull topic to all students. Most of us remember writing "What I Did Last Summer" every fall when we returned to school.

One team of teachers approaches creative writing this way: Their classes gather every Friday morning, and one teacher presents something to the whole group to stimulate their writing. In a letter to parents the teacher stated, "Believe anything your child tells you about Friday morning. It is probably true, no matter how unusual." We do not know exactly what goes on, but we have seen teachers dressed as witches and genies go into that room. One Friday they even brought in a time machine. After the presentation, the students returned to their rooms to write. When the stories are finished, they share them with each other. Spelling, punctuation, and grammar are not corrected at this time. The objective is creative, not stilted, self-conscious writing.

A curriculum geared to each individual is possible for every subject if teachers put in the time and effort to implement it. Although there has not been much done commercially to help them, the music and physical education departments can individualize their curriculums as well as the other departments of the school.

For instance, in music children can work independently or in small groups to learn to play different instruments with the idea of performing at a later date. This is not an easy or a quiet program to administer, but it is more satisfying to children than singing together out of the same book every day.

Occasionally, though, because too much of the same thing is boring, the teacher might want to bring the group together to sing or to play their instruments. Flexibility on the teacher's part is one of the keys to individualization.

The physical education department can individualize its curriculum much like the music department by identifying needs and developing skills from that point. Grouping to teach skills takes the place of the big all-inclusive game where some students always excel and others never succeed. Working in small groups, older or more skillful students, trained by the teacher, can help others develop the skills they need.

Occasionally the teacher will want to bring the group together, as the music teacher does, for a game. Large group games give students a chance to use their new skills and, hopefully, to find success in their achievements. The point is that teachers need to be willing to try something new and different and to consider students' needs before they plan their program.

The physical education teacher at Pitts Elementary School in Denver is working with a pilot program of perceptual motor development that concerns six areas of a kindergartner's physical development.

The children meet with the physical education teacher, the kindergarten teacher, and mother volunteers for a half-hour twice a week. In small groups, the students rotate through a preplanned course of activities such as jumping, crawling, throwing, balance-beam walking, skipping, running, and sliding through small spaces. The premise, supported by educational research, is that gross motor development helps the child manage his body, and fine motor development is conducive to efficiency in activities such as writing, cutting, and painting.

Each student actively participates and improves as he is able. Here the children don't adapt to the program—the program is adapted to the children.

We might mention that some kind of follow-up is as important as the program itself. A first-grade teacher should be told or should see for herself those children who are slow to perfect these physical abilities, for they are the ones who will most likely need a different approach when learning to read or hold a pencil. Problems in the physical education program may signal a learning disability, so it is wise to keep parents informed. Apprise them of their child's progress and ways they can help.

There is also no reason why a physical education program such as this should be confined to the kindergarten. The program can be on-going for children who need additional help or be an integral part of the primary curriculum.

STAFF PATTERNS TO
ENRICH AND IMPROVE THE
INSTRUCTIONAL PROGRAM

*"Teamwork and the
Roles People Play"*

TEAM TEACHING AND DIFFERENTIATED STAFFING ARE "IN," BUT that is not sufficient reason to incorporate them into an educational program. Unless a new organizational plan makes a difference in your instructional program, unless it allows teachers opportunities to create richer, more stimulating learning experiences for children, you might as well stay with the traditional pattern of one teacher teaching one class.

Staffing patterns, like designers' patterns, should be one of a kind, designed for and tailored to fit an individual school. How you organize will depend upon whether you are a large or small school, upon the talents and training of the teachers involved, and upon what the teachers themselves want to do.

In one elementary school teaching teams were organized according to grades. There was a first-grade team, a second-grade team, and so on. However, there was only one kindergarten teacher. She taught two sessions, one in the morning and one in the afternoon. She was overweight, and she often joked about it, but when a district publication inadvertently referred to the kindergarten "team" in that school, she said she knew she was heavy, but she didn't think she weighed enough to be regarded as a "team."

The term "team teaching" means different things to different people. To some, team teaching means two teachers in the same room at the same time. To others it means two or three teachers in a large open space working together with a large group of students. They may divide themselves into smaller groups, but all consider themselves part of the whole.

In some situations teachers have interpreted team teaching to mean "turn teaching." They take turns. One teacher teaches while the other one rests—a waste of time and human resources.

◆ TEAM TEACHING IN SEPARATE ROOMS

The dictionary defines team as two or more horses harnessed to the same vehicle, and that is as good a definition as any for team teaching. Two or more teachers working cooperatively together are a team. They do not have to be in the same room at the same time. Each can teach all subjects in his own classroom, yet through coordination and cooperation be part of the team. The team meets regularly to discuss, plan, and evaluate teaching material and methods.

With the exception of our two multi-age classrooms at the fourth- and fifth-grade level whose teachers team together, and one second-third grade classroom whose teacher teams with the third-grade teachers, we team according to grade sections. Teachers on a team are generally assigned to classrooms in the same area to make cooperation easier.

For example, we have four certified teachers who work together as a team at the third-grade level. They each have their own classroom and their own class, but they do all of their planning together. Early in the year they plan long-range activities, such as which teacher will be responsible for planning and introducing a particular social studies unit. They meet two to three times a week to go over plans and to discuss everything from reading to spelling to creative writing. Each teacher teaches all subjects, and although each child has a homeroom teacher, the children are changed during the day from group to group according to their needs, academic or social.

Organizational plans for teaming partially depend upon the size of the school. Many schools organize grade sections of two or more classes as teams. Smaller schools that have only one section for each grade combine sections of several grades for their teams. Larger schools may have enough sections for two teams at the same grade level, or they might organize several teams of different grade combinations, for instance, kindergarten through third.

One major strength of team teaching is that as teachers plan and work together, invisible walls between them come down. When they discuss units and share ideas, they learn from each other, and curriculum improvement often results.

Another point in favor of team teaching is that it offers teachers and students more grouping options. Children may be assigned to individual teachers, yet move from one room to another for different subjects, depending upon what the team decides is best. If there should be personality conflicts between a student and a teacher, they do not have to suffer with each other all day.

Finally, team teaching gives teachers who have special training, interests, or talents a chance to teach several groups the same subject. For example, one teacher with dramatic training might work with several groups on drama, while another teacher teaches several groups arithmetic or reading.

One criticism of team teaching, as it is sometimes practiced in open space schools, is that the team does not get to know each individual child. He belongs to the group instead of to one teacher. In a school with walls he benefits from team teaching without losing his identity.

The biggest problem with team teaching seems to be personality conflicts that develop between teachers who have to work closely together. If the principal knows of a problem before teams are organized, he can arrange to put teachers who are at odds on different teams, either by moving one teacher up or down a grade level or through cross-grade level teaming.

If a conflict arises after the team is organized, it might help if the principal sits in on team meetings to help reconcile the differences. He can then organize differently the following year or ask one of the teachers to transfer to a different building in the district. Sometimes teachers involved ask for a transfer.

Because of teaming, hiring does not depend solely upon qualifications as it used to. Teachers on a team want some say about with whom they will work, and there is less conflict later on if their opinions are considered. We now not only have to look for a good teacher but for one who can work well with others on a team.

Team teaching can be implemented without differentiated staffing, but planning for team teaching includes planning around teacher leadership. Teams need a leader to give direction, and there are teachers on every staff who exercise sensible judgment, have a sound knowledge of curriculum, and know student needs. They are willing to try something new, and other teachers turn to them for advice. Your teams will accomplish more if you develop an organizational plan, with or without differentiated staffing, whereby these teachers can serve in leadership positions as team leaders, level chairmen, or—as many IGE schools call them—unit leaders. Give them time and opportunity to meet with their teams; then work with them to improve their instructional programs.

There is some disagreement about whether or not to pay team leaders for their added responsibilities. If you pay them above the salary schedule, you risk jealousy and loss of cooperation on the part of the other teachers. If you do not offer incentive pay, the leaders may not be as willing to assume the additional responsibilities.

We have a decentralized budget, so our faculty makes a number of spending decisions. They decided, therefore, not to pay team leaders above the schedule since part of the money set aside for a teacher space would have to be used toward the salary. They did request and were given released time for the team leader, which helps compensate for the added responsibilities the job entails.

When a faculty makes the decision to pay or not to pay, it is not as divisive as if the principal decides and designates the leader.

A job description for the team leaders provides a general framework for their responsibilities, but it need not be limiting since a teaching team needs freedom to plan and teach creatively.

The following position description was developed for our school by the people involved—team leaders, team teachers, and the building principal:

POSITION:
> Team leader

HOW FILLED:
> Elected by the teachers who serve under the unit leader with the approval of the principal.

IMMEDIATE SUPERVISOR:
> Building principal.

TERMS OF APPOINTMENT:
> Serves one full school year.
> May be re-elected the following school year.
> May resign this position for personal reasons.

RATE OF PAY:
> Teacher salary schedule.
> Release time provided to perform necessary duties as worked out by the staff.

REQUIREMENTS:
> Meets all certification requirements of district and state.
> At least two years teaching experience in the school.
> Tenure required.

DESIRED QUALIFICATIONS:
> Master's degree or course work toward a master's degree.

Demonstrated leadership potential.

Demonstrated ability and desire to work toward program improvement.

Ability to get along with others and to help others work together.

RELATIONSHIPS AND DUTIES:

Liaison representative to all unit leaders' meetings.

Liaison between principal and faculty.

Coordinates program with primary or intermediate staff.

Works toward implementation of school philosophy.

Shares ideas with other unit leaders.

Shares ideas with building principal.

Coordinates and shares ideas with special teaching personnel in the building.

Serves on district and school committees.

Works with elementary consultant.

Liaison between team and teacher aides.

Plans staff meetings with building principal.

Works on school schedule.

Helps in setting up new programs, such as the art center.

Has part, when possible, in recommending teachers to fill vacancies on the team.

Suggests ideas for faculty meeting programs.

Coordinates special student programs that are planned within the building or unit.

Participates as a full-time team member.

Guides team members in selecting materials and educational experiences that are suitable for the needs of their students.

Serves on the Instructional Improvement Committee.

Is responsible for communicating decisions of the Instructional Improvement Committee to the unit staff.

If you feel such a job description is too structured to suit your needs, simply designate a leader to meet with you once a week and to meet with the team once a week to plan and discuss team activities.

◆ DIFFERENTIATED STAFFING

Differentiated staffing is a sophisticated form of team teaching involving defined teaching roles and the use of paraprofessionals to relieve teachers of non-teaching duties. The organizational pattern involves a hierarchy of teachers, student teachers, and aides.

Differentiated staffing is controversial for two reasons: *(1)* some plans call for a differentiated pay scale, and *(2)* some feel that positions that would otherwise be filled by certified teachers are being filled by aides for less money.

We believe a certified teacher should teach, but much of the teacher's day is devoted to non-teaching tasks that could just as well be performed by paraprofessionals. Teacher aides and interns can reinforce skills already taught, do clerical work, and perform various supervisory tasks as well as teachers. Allocated dollars hire more paraprofessionals than they do teachers. The more people there are working with children, the more chances there are to individualize instruction. In some districts it is the teacher organizations that have seen the advantages of differentiation, and they are the ones pushing for it through negotiations.

Those who are against any move toward differentiated staffing because they believe it is going to displace teachers need to consider whether it is the business of the school to provide children with the best education possible for the money spent or whether it is to provide jobs for teachers.

Starting a differentiated program in a traditional school with the one-teacher-per-class organizational pattern may seem like an impossibility, and it will be unless something or someone makes it happen. Like a trickle of water that breaks through a crack in a dam to become a torrent, there has to be an opening before differentiated staffing can begin.

For us two cracks appeared at the same time. First, the teacher organization asked for (and the district negotiated) duty-free lunch periods for teachers. This opening allowed us to hire paid supervisory aides, and once teachers had seen their value, the flow increased.

Second, according to district allotment, we were to have 27.6 teacher spaces for our staffing next year. (By staffing we mean the number of certificated positions.) Of course it is impossible to hire .6 of a person, but .6 did mean a certain dollar figure. In this case .6 equalled $6,000. With that figure in mind, the faculty knew we could hire four instructional aides for four hours at $2 an hour, and that is what they decided to do.

Now we differentiate the equivalent of 1.2 to 2.0 positions each year for aide positions ranging from technician to student assistant. Money for one teacher space is calculated on an average of the teacher salaries in the district. As the teacher salary schedule increases, so does the average from which to work.

Aides are paid according to an established district salary schedule, and since the staff itself decided not to differentiate the team leader's salary, we do not depart from the salary schedule when it comes to certificated teacher pay. There is differentiation through the salary schedule because, theoretically, teachers on tenure and at the top of the schedule are receiving more money for their knowledge and experience.

Jumping into differentiated staffing without knowing what you are getting into would be like a parachutist jumping from a plane not knowing whether or not his chute will open; in both cases the results could be disastrous. Pre-planning is essential.

Most people who have had experience with differentiated staffing would agree that teachers must be the ones to plan their differentiated staffing pattern since it is their roles and their tasks that are being differentiated. Planning includes the consideration of the following points: (1) differentiated roles, (2) definition of responsibilities, (3) flexible scheduling, and (4) salary range differential.

At first you may not want to differentiate more than three roles—team leader, teacher, and aide—although some schools that have been differentiating for a longer period of time have incorporated other positions, such as teacher intern. To divide tasks and avoid overlapping responsibilities and resulting conflicts, our district publishes the following role definitions:

Unit or Team Leader: The primary function of the leader is to coordinate all activities within the team. This person is responsible for implementing the curriculum and the teaching-learning plan of students assigned to the team and for coordinating team activities for the team, school, and district. He meets regularly with the principal and other unit leaders to help make decisions regarding more than his team.

Teacher: The primary function of the teacher is to guide and help each student under his charge to achieve his maximum individual potential. This requires each teacher to individualize the separate and distinct components of the learning cycle, namely: preassessment, objective setting, teaching program, and assessment. The teacher must subordinate teaching to learning and be prepared to use a wide variety of human and nonhuman resources to achieve this end.

Incumbents serve as full contributing members of a team and are directly responsible to the team leader and through him, to all other team members. The incumbent also supervises trainees and noncertificated personnel. About ninety per cent of the teacher's work day is spent in direct contact with students.

Teacher Intern: Teacher interns are specially certified, paid, fifth-year teacher trainees working on advanced degrees and receiving preservice training experiences and professional on-the-job evaluation. The intern's work is supervised by the team leader and other appropriate training personnel, but they serve as full-time, contributing members of the team with a minimum and decreasing amount of direction. Incumbents may supervise noncertificated personnel. Incumbents perform essentially the same duties as those of a professional teacher, but only as increased competency is demonstrated. Work load accounts for eighty per cent and college training twenty per cent of the total work year. Incumbents are paid commensurate with this amount of work load and level of training. Upon completion of their training, which is in conjunction with colleges of education, incumbents are qualified for a regular teaching certificate.

Instructional Aide: Instructional aides complete preservice training and a one-year internship designed to prepare them to be paraprofessional assistants to the teams. Incumbents are certified as paraprofessional instructional aides and are paid commensurate with this training, experience, and responsibility.

The primary function of the instructional aide is to provide skilled assistance to the team to which he is assigned. This assistance generally falls within the scope of the learning cycle for children. These tasks, however, never assume the full characteristics or responsibilities of the professional teacher. Nevertheless, they are closely related to the teaching-learning activities of the team. Incumbents work under supervision of the team.

Team Aide: Team aides complete a preservice training program at the beginning of the year and take part in other in-service activities in addition to whatever other training they may have already had.

The team aide's primary function is to assist the team with clerical, housekeeping, and general support duties within a classroom and school setting. This may include supervision of the lunchroom or the playground. Team aides work under the direction of the principal and other team personnel.

◆ USING AIDES EFFECTIVELY

Some teachers fear that having an aide will take more of their time than it will save because they will have to plan for the aide as well as for their class. Unless there is preservice training for the aide and organization on the part of the team, this could be true.

A short training program for beginning aides saves teacher time in the long run and helps prevent problems during the course of the year. In some cases, the district trains the aides; in others, training is left to the principal and the staff. A training program should include orientation on school policies, especially those regarding student discipline, use of equipment, office procedures, and team and staff expectations. A first-aid course is particularly necessary for playground aides.

Keeping aides busy at meaningful tasks is largely a matter of team planning. Some teams give the aide certain regular duties as listed in the job description, such as collecting and counting lunch money or running off dittos; then when the aide sits in on planning meetings, other duties are assigned on a daily or weekly basis.

Most aides are not under contract as teachers are, and their salaries are not high, so there is a high rate of turnover. If they find a better job, they take it. When hiring, it helps to ask for a verbal commitment, but there is no way of keeping them. We don't have a solution for this problem, but even though it is difficult to make a midterm change, our staff would rather work with aides than without them.

To improve relationships and keep the lines of communication open, involve aides, or at least one aide who represents the others, in faculty meetings as well as team meetings. Remember, too, that they are part of the staff and as such should be included in staff activities.

Not all teams have full-time aides. When an aide must be shared, teams can best work out the time division amongst themselves. One team may want an aide an hour a day for the week, while another may prefer to have the hours accumulate until an aide can be with them a full day.

A job description for aides sets guidelines for the team to follow and covers such points as title, immediate supervisor, hiring, rate of pay, working relationships and assigned duties. The following example may be adapted to fit a particular situation:

POSITION:
Teacher Aide and Supervisory Aide K-6.

APPOINTED BY:
The central personnel office upon recommendation of the building principal.

IMMEDIATE SUPERVISOR:
Building principal delegates responsibility to unit leader.

RATE OF PAY:
As per district schedule for teacher aides.

REQUIREMENTS:

Typing ability.
Ability to work with teachers and office personnel.
Ability to learn how to operate various office machines.
Knowledge of first aid.

RELATIONSHIPS:

Works with and cooperates with teachers through unit leaders.
Works with and shares ideas with other teacher aides.
Takes some direction, only as necessary, from building principal.
Shares ideas and cooperates with school secretaries.

DUTIES:

Collects lunch money.
Supervises lunchroom or playground.
Types and runs dittos for teachers.
Keeps attendance records.
Guides independent study, enrichment, and remedial work set up by the teacher.
Checks notebooks, corrects papers, and supervises testing and makeup work.
Keeps art supply levels constant.
Assists with reading and storytelling.
Does bookkeeping as required.
Assists in developing instructional group records and schedules.
Assists in preparing class displays and bulletin boards.
Cares for laboratory and other instructional equipment.
Helps students with hats, coats, overshoes, and so forth.
Accepts other non-teaching duties as assigned.

EVALUATION:

Performance of this job will be evaluated annually by the principal with the assistance of the unit leader.

It may seem strange that the principal evalutes, when the aide works with the team and is responsible to the unit leader. Teachers, however, are often reluctant to do an evaluation because of the close working relationship they have with their aides, and they would rather the principal take the final responsibility.

ENLISTING THE HELP OF VOLUNTEERS AND STUDENT ASSISTANTS

"People Galore"
❖❖❖❖❖

IN THE DAYS OF THE ONE-ROOM SCHOOLHOUSE IT WAS POSSIBLE for high school graduates to obtain teaching positions. One who did tells of being hired at age nineteen to teach grades one through eight. The first day of school he looked at the first graders and realized he didn't have any idea of how to teach a child to read. The students had double desks, so instead of having eighth graders sit by eighth graders, he sat first graders by seventh and eighth graders, and at the end of the first year the first graders could read.

He probably went too far because aides and volunteers should assist, not teach, but he did use older students to help teach younger students.

There must have been others in the same situation who did the same thing. The idea of students and volunteers assisting the teacher is not new, but planning programs to include them is. Modern schools are utilizing parent volunteers and secondary school students in innovative ways to improve the program and to individualize instruction.

◆ ADULT VOLUNTEERS IN THE SCHOOL PROGRAM

Despite recent criticism of volunteer programs that maintains if a job is worth doing, the person doing it should be paid, volunteer programs in the schools are growing. Benefits work both ways. Volunteers find a meaningful outlet without being burdened by full-time job responsibilities, and schools' instructional programs are enriched and improved through volunteer help. Most schools do not have the money to pay for the services volunteers donate. If they had to pay, they would have to do without.

Adult volunteers not only save teacher time and district money, they foster and improve school-community relations. Barriers between the schools and the public crumble as the schools involve the community in their programs. One principal, who is deeply committed to a volunteer program, admits that he used to feel threatened when parents came to school. He thought they were there to find fault. Now, after several years of volunteer help, he has changed his mind. He says, "Instead of trying to convince parents that everything we do is right, we don't mind letting them see that we make mistakes, because they can also see that essentially what we are doing is good."

Another principal states that the ease with which his district passes bond issues since they have had volunteers in the schools proves the wisdom of letting the public in on school business. In that district volunteers even handle the bond issue publicity. People are often critical when they don't know what's going on, but those who are involved and who believe in what they are doing have a positive attitude that helps sell the school program to others.

Sometimes volunteers in the building see a need for equipment or supplies and put forth extra effort to obtain what the school should have. When a volunteer in our health room saw that we needed new health room furniture, she obtained it for us. A volunteer in another building found the school wanted a sewing machine for the learning center, so she donated hers.

We have approximately sixty volunteers working throughout the school in six different programs. Possibly because of the careful organization by those who planned the programs, we have not had any major problems in connection with any of the volunteers. Without the services they provide, we would not be able to individualize to the extent that we have. Descriptions of our programs follow:

LIBRARY VOLUNTEERS

A chairman working with the school librarian started our first volunteer program by organizing twenty people to help in the library. They come in on a regular basis to help shelve books, check books in and out, update the picture file, and process library materials. The volunteers and the chairman change from year to year, but the program is ongoing. As a result, the library is well organized, and the librarian is free to spend more time with children.

RIGHT TO READ

As an outgrowth of the national right to read effort, we have implemented a right to read program involving volunteers. After a short training and orientation course organized by a volunteer chairman and taught by a district teacher, volunteers work with small groups of children under a teacher's direction to reinforce reading skills.

RIGHT TO MATH

One of our teachers adapted the right to read idea and organized volunteers to work with his team in the area of math. He carefully planned ways parents could help children; then he met with and trained the volunteers himself. Under his direction the volunteers work with small groups, and in one-to-one situations use games or whatever materials are necessary to reinforce math concepts. He asked the parents involved for comments at the end of the year, and they reacted positively. One said she learned more than she taught. Another said she had been mystified by new math, but now she understood it and was pleased that she knew what her child was doing. As a bonus, children liked to have their parents in the classroom.

HEALTH ROOM VOLUNTEERS

Our school does not employ a full-time nurse. The nurse divides her time among several schools, so previously the principal and the secretary took care of children who became ill or who were injured when the nurse was not there. The nurse helped us organize volunteers to provide full-time coverage in the health room during school hours. Some volunteers are former nurses; others qualify through a first-aid course. Since our health room is close to the office, the volunteers help the school secretary when they aren't busy in the health room.

ROOM MOTHERS

We have room mothers who differ from classroom volunteers in that they work with the teachers through the parent organization. For organizational purposes, they are the contact between teachers and parents. They help organize school parties, help supervise field trips, and make phone calls when it is necessary to reach all parents in a room.

CLASSROOM VOLUNTEERS

Assisting individual teachers in whatever ways the teacher wishes, classroom volunteers tutor small groups or individuals or, depending on their talents and abilities, direct a play, plan a creative writing project, or demonstrate watercolor painting. They come on a regular basis or for a one-time-only presentation of a trip, hobby, job, or experience.

If teachers doubt the value of volunteers, start on a small scale, as we did in the library, with a teacher willing to work with them. If the program is successful, enthusiasm is contagious and spreads throughout the school.

Once teachers decide they want volunteers, the first step in organizing a program is to recruit one volunteer, a dedicated person able to spend a great deal of time, to coordinate it. Working through the parent organization, either one chairman heads a committee that oversees all volunteer programs, or different chairmen are selected to head each different program. Chairmen then recruit volunteers through the school paper, the local paper, word of mouth, or local service organizations. One school recruits at a big coffee klatsch where parents are asked to sign up for the job they want to do. This same school is careful to call every parent who signs up, so word won't get around that the school says it needs volunteers but it doesn't really care. Whether or not you screen volunteers depends upon the size of the school and how well you know the parents. Sometimes it is necessary; sometimes it is not.

Recruiting volunteer help is more difficult in low income areas, because mothers who are home can't afford to pay baby sitters, and those who are working don't have the time. It might be possible to organize a nursery at school for the mothers of small children, or you might look beyond the parents to the community for help.

One school has a housing project for retired persons near the school. The volunteer chairman organized a program to involve these people and give them an opportunity to be of service. For example, a retired banker helped a class learn about the country's economic structure. Because of his business experience and background, he knew more about the subject than the teacher, and the children benefited because he shared his knowledge with them. Teachers note that these retired people are dependable and conscientious. They hardly ever miss a day. If they say they are going to be there, they are there, on time.

There should be training programs for volunteers just as there are for aides. Depending upon what they are doing, they may only need a short orientation course, but some kind of training program will save teacher time and prevent conflicts later.

Turnover and absenteeism are often the biggest problems in a volunteer program and are prime reasons teachers give ͟ ͟ ͟ ͟ ͟ such a program in the first place. Asking for a ͟ ͟ ͟ ͟ for the year at the beginning cuts down the ͟ ͟ ͟ and asking a volunteer to train a replacement when a situation makes it impossible for him to continue makes the transition easier. Substitutes keep the program running smoothly when a volunteer has to be absent. Nothing is more upsetting to teachers than to depend on a volunteer who does not show up.

Volunteers, though, need to be assigned meaningful tasks, or they come to feel that it doesn't make any difference whether they are there or not. A volunteer in a little room cutting out letters for the bulletin board might think that she would be better off at home doing her ironing. Volunteers do not have to be involved in classroom activities but in some task they know counts.

In some states, Pennsylvania, for example, what volunteers or noncertificated personnel can or can't do is spelled out in state laws. The laws limit volunteers' duties, but if teams or an individual teacher plan and coordinate volunteer help, they can give the volunteers meaningful tasks that do not conflict with those of certificated teachers.

Volunteers, particularly chairmen, deserve recognition for their contributions. Special coffee sessions, a personal thanks, a thank-you note, or a public thank-you published in the school paper are ways to let them know their efforts are appreciated.

Adult volunteer programs are limited only by the energy the staff is willing to expend in implementing the programs and by the number of people willing to volunteer.

◆ HOW SECONDARY STUDENTS LEARN AS THEY ASSIST IN ELEMENTARY SCHOOLS

When secondary and elementary school teachers and principals cooperate to develop a program in which secondary students help teach elementary students, everybody benefits.

High school students gain knowledge and understanding of subject matter, their own desires and limitations, and how children learn and develop. Elementary children profit from individualized instruction and close interpersonal relationships with the high school students who assist them. Teachers benefit by interacting with students from different grade levels and by the help they receive with instructional and clerical tasks.

Student help may range from one student listening to another read for a short period of time to a more complex two- or three-day-a-week program that gives high school students credits toward graduation. The historical precedents of such activities and the wide range of current possibilities, especially the variety of Youth Tutoring Youth Programs throughout the United States, are described in *Children Teach Children* by Alan Gartner, Mary Kohler, and Frank Riessman (New York: Harper & Row, 1971).

Two programs that have proven themselves effective in our district and our school are SAT (Students Assisting Teachers) and MAL (Mutually Aided Learning). The MAL program is associated with a subject area, such as math, science, language arts, and even swimming. The SAT program covers general classwork and is not as structured. Although these two programs are different, each gives high school students a chance to work with elementary children.

The primary aim of the SAT program is involvement of the student assistant in the teaching-learning process. Student assistants are assigned to a cooperating teacher who must be willing to give them varied experiences, most of which involve them with other students. Student assistants receive one-half of one credit for a semester's work, which must add up to at least sixty hours. They may earn up to one full credit during the year. Duties of a student assistant may include:

◇   Help children take care of plants and animals.

◇   Assist children with clothing at recess, noontime, or dismissal.

◇ Grade papers, reproduce materials, and file or record information.

◇ Conduct individual or group drill work.

◇ Help students with unfinished classwork.

◇ Prepare bulletin boards, teaching devices, and the like.

◇ Collect data, maps, graphs, books, and other materials for a specific lesson.

◇ Help supervise the class during study periods, library periods, in the lunchroom, and on the playground.

◇ Assist with class programs or small group presentations.

◇ Develop and present simple lessons or short units of study to small groups of children with the assistance and consent of the cooperating teacher who retains responsibility for all instruction.

◇ Pass out and collect materials.

◇ Help students put materials away and keep the classroom in order.

◇ Assist children who have been absent with the classwork they missed.

◇ Read stories to children or listen to the children read stories.

◇ Observe the cooperating teacher use various instructional techniques and classroom procedures.

One administrator or program coordinator at the high school is responsible for the SAT program in our district. The district spells out his responsibilities as follows:

◇ Identify schools and teachers in the district who would like to have student assistants.

◇ Recruit and interview high school students who would like to assist teachers in the district.

◇ Process and assign student applicants to teachers requesting student assistants.

◇ Inform the student assistants and cooperating teachers of their respective duties and responsibilities and the procedures that should be followed to accomplish the goals and objectives of the SAT program.

◇ Conduct weekly feedback sessions for the student assistants to help them learn how to become an effective assistant and how to develop a good working relationship with teachers and children.

◇ Visit each student assistant on the job at least once each quarter and confer with his cooperating teacher about his observed capability and reliability as a student assistant.

◇ Participate in the evaluation and reassignment procedure, including reading the cooperating teacher's evaluation and the student assistant's final report and recording the grade the student assistant should receive.

◇ Disseminate information about the SAT program to interested students, teachers, and parents.

The principal's responsibilities concerning the program are as follows:

◇ Explain any school policies or rules to the assistant which pertain to him and to the staff.

◇ Acquaint the student assistant with school facilities and the staff with whom he will be working.

◇ Arrange to keep a record of the student assistant's attendance in the school office.

The main emphasis in the MAL program is individualizing the elementary learning program. High school students, called learning assistants, are trained by a high school teacher in subject matter and techniques of working with small groups of younger students. They come to the elementary school to work with elementary students in a specific subject area such as science.

The high school teacher and the elementary teacher plan together the objectives and activities for the semester. Although the high school students are enrolled in a high school class and receive credit for their work, when they are at the elementary school, they work under the direction of the elementary teacher.

Letter writing is a language arts activity that offers opportunity for this kind of small group instruction. We know that elementary students in the same grade have different knowledge and letter writing capabilities. By pre-assessing student skills and by regrouping according to what students need to learn, each group can work on a different aspect of letter writing. One learning assistant might teach format, while another learning assistant works with letter content, or yet another teaches the difference between a business and a social letter.

MAL is one of the innovations we tried first on a pilot basis. A fifth-grade team of three teachers volunteered to participate, and a high school science teacher trained fifteen to twenty students to help the team individualize their science program. The students worked with groups of four to five younger students on different science projects during the semester, and the teachers involved felt that the students' help had improved the program.

In the beginning, although MAL had been planned on paper, problems such as transportation, student evaluation, use of materials, and coordinated scheduling did come up and had to be solved within the three classes. We worked out the "bugs," and during the following year, the program grew to take in other grade levels and other subject areas.

Many of the students who volunteer for MAL and SAT do so because they think they want to be teachers. These programs give them a chance to find out whether or not they like to work with children over an extended period of time.

◆ STUDENTS ASSISTING STUDENTS

Programs that involve high school students with the elementary schools take a lot of planning and coordination, mainly because of scheduling and transportation problems. On a less formal basis, students can assist students within the same school.

This type of program does not involve a great deal of organization. An exchange of students may simply be worked out between two teachers or two teams at a time that is convenient to both of them.

Some schools have organized this so fourth, fifth, and sixth graders go to listen to first and second graders read. Not necessarily do just the top students participate, for it builds ego when students, who always needed help themselves, help someone else for a change. There are advantages both ways. Sometimes the one who is helping learns as much or more than the one who is being helped. One fourth-grade boy told his teacher, after listening to a first grader read, "He read pretty good. In fact, he reads better'n me."

FLEXIBLE SCHEDULING FOR A FLEXIBLE PROGRAM

"Timely Advice"

❖❖❖❖

A NUMBER OF YEARS AGO THE TELEPHONE RANG; AN UPSET father was on the other end of the line. It seemed that the time his child's class was scheduled to use the lavatory didn't coincide with the child's natural habits.

That particular problem was worked out, and we don't receive calls on this subject anymore. It has been quite a while since classes at our school lined up to go to the lavatory at the same time. Children leave the classrooms when they have to because in scheduling, as in everything else, we are taking individual differences into account.

Flexible scheduling, as we conceive it, does not mean modular scheduling. According to one dictionary definition, flexible means "responsive to or readily adjustable to changing conditions." That is the kind of scheduling we are trying to effect within our walls.

You can't have a flexible program if you don't have a flexible schedule. Teachers locked into a rigid schedule where bells ring on the hour are not free to work within the time limits they think best. Instead of the schedule serving them, they are bound to the schedule. Even principals can become so involved in making and administering schedules that they don't have time to be the instructional leaders they should be.

Departmentalization, usually at the upper intermediate level, provides the least amount of schedule flexibility, while the self-contained classroom offers the most. When we changed to team teaching, we did so knowing that we were sacrificing some of the flexibility we had with the self-contained classroom. Teachers working alone had the option of teaching subjects when they wanted to for as long as they thought necessary. They only had to work their daily class routine around the times they had signed up for music or physical education.

Anytime, however, that more than one person is involved in the child's instruction, some kind of a schedule becomes necessary. The more people involved, the more complicated it becomes.

♦ SCHEDULING FOR TEAM TEACHING

If teachers are teaming and trying to individualize instruction, they need individual and group planning time. To plan together a team's planning hours must coincide, so classes belonging to the same team have to be somewhere else at the same time. One class might go to physical education, one to music, and another to library, or two might go to physical education and one to music. It doesn't matter what the arrangement is as long as all the classes are gone at once.

One way to provide three teachers a half-hour planning time together is to schedule three special classes at the same time with each class having a different special each day. For example, a class would have library, music, and physical education, then start over with library on the fourth day. A sample schedule follows:

First week 9:30–10:00

	M	T	W	Th	F
A	P.E.	Lib.	Mu.	P.E.	Lib.
B	Mu.	P.E.	Lib.	Mu.	P.E.
C	Lib.	Mu.	P.E.	Lib.	Mu.

Second week 9:30–10:00

	M	T	W	Th	F
A	Mu.	P.E.	Lib.	Mu.	P.E.
B	Lib.	Mu.	P.E.	Lib.	Mu.
C	P.E.	Lib.	Mu.	P.E.	Lib.

Teams also have to schedule for group instruction. For instance, if a team of four teachers assigned one hundred to one hundred and twenty students wanted to group them for math, all those students would need to have math at the same time. The amount of time allotted and when the team wants it may vary from week to week, and that is up to the team to decide. However, the time for music and physical education has to be determined because these department schedules involve the whole school. Therefore, the team must work around that schedule.

Devising a master plan satisfactory to all the teams is like putting together a jigsaw puzzle and trying to make all the odd-shaped pieces fit.

◆ INVOLVING TEACHERS IN SCHEDULE PLANNING

We prefer to let teachers do the scheduling and resolve their own conflicts rather than schedule through administrative dictates. The principal does need to sit in on the planning, however, because scheduling involves variables that only he may know.

We have a committee that meets in the spring to work out the schedule for the following school year. The special teachers, such as music, physical education, speech, and library, serve on the committee along with a representative from each team. In a smaller school the committee might include the entire faculty.

The first step is to identify the factors that affect the schedule, such as the length of the lunch period, the maximum number of children who can eat lunch at any one time, the number of special teachers available to the staff, how often special subjects are offered during a week's time, the number of supervisory aides available, what and when facilities such as the gymnasiums are available, and, of course, the beginning and ending of the school day. When the teachers sit down to work out the master schedule, each should have a copy of the factors that will influence it.

Some teachers have fixed ideas about when a subject should be taught. For example, many think that the only time to teach reading is the first thing in the morning. (Research, however, does not bear this out.) If every teacher in the school taught reading at the beginning of the school day, no one would be going to physical education or music classes at that time. Obviously, then the staff must compromise.

Team representatives know what their teachers want, and the committee knows what the constraints are, so, with some give and take on everyone's part, the schedule can be worked out. If, however, some problems can't be resolved by the teachers themselves and the group has come to an impasse, the principal will have to make a final decision in light of what is best for all.

There is hardly enough time to work out a master schedule before or after school. Therefore, dismiss the students for a half day, if this is possible in your district, or hire substitutes for the team representatives and have teachers keep their children instead of sending them to special classes while scheduling is in progress. This way those involved will have an uninterrupted period of time to work out a schedule that is to everybody's advantage.

Even though the schedule is down on paper, dittoed, mimeographed, or typed, it should still be flexible. Changes occur during the course of the school year, so if the need arises, don't hesitate to change the schedule accordingly.

We made such a change when we had a scheduling problem with the three first-grade teachers. The only time open for them to send their classes to music and physical education came at the time they wanted to teach reading.

To solve the problem, they decided to teach their own P.E. and music at a time they preferred. One teacher had a musical background and played the piano, another had taught elementary P.E., and the third had taken some college P.E. courses; therefore they were qualified to do this. They organized seventy students so that two-thirds had P.E. while one-third had music. Each child had P.E. for two days, then one day of music, then the cycle started over again.

Their plan suited the administration because the special teachers were overloaded, and it alleviated the situation. The first-grade teachers did need planning time, though, and they didn't have it. We worked on the problem and were finally able to give them an additional aide half an hour a day to supervise morning recess while they planned. Meantime the regular P.E. and music teachers juggled their schedules to make time during the lunch hour for intramural sports and choir.

All seemed well, but it didn't last. About the middle of January the first-grade teachers began to feel the pressure and asked to be relieved. Now it was too late to go back to the original plan because it would disrupt other classes, so we had to work out something else.

During that semester the school population had increased by twenty-five students. Since the growth justified additional staff, we hired a part-time high school P.E. teacher for an additional hour to take over first-grade P.E. and a part-time music aide to assist the music teacher. Class size increased, but time periods remained the same as when the first-grade teachers taught their own special classes. Thus the program continued to function smoothly.

◆ MODULAR SCHEDULING

One principal tells visitors that his school has modular scheduling. What the school really has are the same blocks of time it always had, but they are called mods now instead of periods. Modular scheduling involves more than calling a period a mod. It is a method of scheduling whereby the school day is divided into small segments of time and appropriate amounts of time are devoted to each subject area. Actually modular scheduling is done within teams when they plan and allot different amounts of time for each subject.

One traditionally built school adopted a modular plan for intermediate students that worked in the following way. Each child received a weekly schedule compiled by a computer. Subject areas were divided into half-hour mods, and students were scheduled for classes forty to sixty per cent of their day. The remaining time was left open so they might select other areas of interest. Each day's schedule was different, so the printout told the child where to go and for how long. Some classes lasted one mod, while others ran for two or three.

When a teacher had free time for students, a signal, such as a green light outside the classroom door, was turned on. This indicated students were free to come in if they had the time and so desired. The same signaling technique was used by all teachers, including the librarian.

The modular schedule has strengths, especially for the child who is an independent learner and mature enough to handle the freedom that such a program provides. Children who need structure and teacher guidance generally have some trouble with modular scheduling.

Principals we talked to who have tried modular scheduling said that initiating it caused more conflict between teachers and more problems with parents than any other innovation—possibly because it affected the whole school.

Also, contrary to what many educators believe, in some ways modular scheduling is inflexible. Because children are not together for more than one mod, if a teacher wishes to do something different with a class, say take a field trip beyond the scheduled time, the children miss other classes going on with business as usual.

Modular scheduling is supposed to give smaller student groups and more teacher planning time. The Ford Foundation reports, however, that in its Comprehensive School Improvement Program it found the degree of flexibility almost directly related to the percentage of free time during the day allotted to independent study. Without exception, it said, questions of student autonomy and discipline were raised by granting free time.

We are not considering modular scheduling at our school because the teachers already have the freedom to plan any kind of schedule they wish within their teams, even to allowing students some free time. We feel school-wide modular scheduling would not benefit us enough at this time to compensate for the problems it would create.

◆ FUN DAYS AND FULL YEARS

Thanks to the creativity of teachers planning together, as many schedules can be developed as there are teams planning together. In our school district's thirteen elementary schools, there are thirteen different school-wide scheduling plans.

Some schools schedule so students earn free time through classwork for cultural, interest, or hobby activities, usually on a Friday afternoon. Others have an extended day where students come early or stay late either for extra help or for extended day activity classes such as macramé, Spanish, or whatever else students and teachers plan.

One Denver school that still has specific periods of time for classes because of departmentalization has shortened those periods to make extra time at the end of the day. Students may either go home then or stay for activities. More stay than go home, and these classes are different because students are there by choice, not chance.

Summit County schools, located in a Colorado ski area, dismiss classes every Friday afternoon so students can go to the slopes. Their schedule does what all schedules should do—meets the needs of the students involved.

More and more school districts are scheduling year-round school. In the beginning overcrowding and lack of space forced the move, but now educators recognize other values in it. There is some reason to believe, and educators are studying the premise, that students make more progress without a long summer vacation in which to forget what they have learned. Others argue for the family vacation options year-round school provides, while still others see it as a way to help outside recreation agencies such as the "Y" make full year-round use of their facilities.

Looking to the future, if the present birth rate trend continues, zero population growth is possible. No one knows for certain what will happen, but it is conceivable that in a few years the number of school buildings will be more than adequate to serve children of school age. Year-round school, therefore, is a way to accommodate the children we now have until the trend becomes clear.

We have started a year-round program with one class of kindergartners at our school. It came about when the kindergarten enrollment grew to sixty-six before school started, with a projected increase to seventy-six by the end of the year. This number was too high for the two kindergarten sections we have always had, so we offered the parents the following alternatives:

1. Stay with the traditional plan for two sections. The classes would be large, but we would have aides to help.

2. Go to triple sessions. The classes would be small but would meet for two instead of two and one-half hours.

3. Bus students to another school. We would keep the first fifty registered and send the overflow of sixteen to twenty-five students to another school.

4. Extend the school year from July 9th through June 26th
    of the following year on a 45-15 plan (forty-five days
    of school—fifteen days of vacation).

Some parents were enthusiastic about an extended school
year; others were anything but. One probably voiced what
others were thinking when she said it would interfere with
her life style. Consequently, we decided to have a traditional calendar for those who wanted it, and an extended
year calendar for those who wanted that. The traditional
class had thirty-four students, while the year-round class
had thirty-two. However, since one-fourth of the year-
round class would always be on vacation, only twenty-four
children would be in the classroom at the same time. If the
school population grows as predicted, we will add another
section, either traditional or year-round as parents dictate.

In this case not only did scheduling school for a summer
session alleviate crowded conditions, it offered the further
advantages of outdoor educational experiences and free,
unscheduled use of other school facilities such as the
gymnasium.

MAKING THE LIBRARY
SERVE
THE WHOLE SCHOOL

"More Than a Book Depository"
❖❖❖❖

WHILE NEW SCHOOLS CALL THEIR LIBRARIES MEDIA CENTERS
and their librarians media specialists, teachers in older
schools find it difficult to call the library and the librarian
by any other name. Teachers may refer to the smaller centers
around the school as media centers because they are new,
but generally the library is still the library and the person
in charge is still the librarian.

The name may be the same, but the concept is different.
No longer a quiet sanctuary where a stern librarian guards
the books, the new school library is a lively place. A hum
of activity replaces the shush of imposed silence. At any
one time students may be reading in a carrel, listening to
tapes, viewing filmstrips or continuous film loops, browsing
for books, or researching material. The library and the
smaller media centers are more than book depositories;
they are the hub of the learning wheel.

A library media program is not a place, a person, or a
collection, much as school management is not the principal
or the school office. It is a concept. In both cases, facilities,
personnel, and money are needed, but each factor alone
does not constitute the concept.

As an integrated part of the total school program, rather
than a unit apart or complete in itself, the new library

concept should serve the school in a new way. The librarian works as a resource person in cooperation with teachers and teams to coordinate library resources with teacher needs.

A librarian who has formerly been a successful classroom teacher in the district knows the curriculum and is better able to understand the kind of help teachers need and to give them that help. Making the librarian a member of the school's curriculum committees and arranging for her to meet periodically with the teams keeps her attuned to teachers' needs. She might well be considered the fifth member of each four-member team.

Teacher-librarian cooperation works both ways, for teachers as well as librarians need to be involved in planning for media materials, evaluating resources, motivating library use, and implementing the media program.

Study carrels, carpeting, and beanbag chairs are pleasant to have but in themselves don't change anything. It is the cooperation and communication between the teachers and the librarian that bring change.

In our school, teachers ask the librarian to assemble materials ahead of time for units of study. Then when the class needs the material, it is ready. The librarian, meantime, helps the teachers gather pictures from the picture file for bulletin board displays and suggests films and filmstrips to go along with the unit. When children from that class come for materials, the librarian knows their reading level and suggests appropriate books. She is alert to what the class is studying and lets the teacher know when she comes across items that will enrich the unit.

The goal and purpose of the library media center and the librarian's major function is to improve instruction by coordinating library resources with classroom teaching objectives. In addition, the librarian is responsible for teaching library skills and organizing and dispersing library materials, but working with the teachers to improve instruction has top priority.

To facilitate such a cooperative effort, Mason Ridge Elementary School in the Parkway School District in St. Louis, Missouri, developed a guide to its curriculum materials. One teacher from each grade level, the librarian, and the guidance counselor worked at a paid workshop during the winter putting together a guide that coordinated what the teachers wanted to teach with library materials available. They used a horizontal format that provided room on the paper to list the unit or skill on the left side and the materials available on the right. That way they could read it across without having to turn pages.

If you are to have an effective library media program, you need to establish with your librarian and your teachers what they want and hire accordingly. If they want a place to store books and equipment and someone to keep track of them and check them out, an aide or volunteer can probably do the job, but if they want an integrated school program, there is no substitute for a fully-trained, qualified person who has had classroom teaching experience and who knows curriculum and children as well as she knows media materials.

If allocation or approval has to come through the central office, work with it to create a position. If there is no money, you might increase teacher-pupil ratio by a vote of the faculty and hire a librarian in place of a teacher.

This job, as we have defined it, is too much for one person to handle, so you need to devise ways to give the librarian help. We use a number of parent and student volunteers who work under the librarian's direction to pull materials for a class, shelve books, take care of check-outs, make repairs, and type cards. A student volunteer program not only helps the librarian, it teaches students library skills as they put library principles into practice. Paid aides and college interns are other possibilities.

Schools that have good programs going have personnel willing to move ahead and try something new. Schools that don't are limited by their personnel, not their walls.

There need be no relationship between the age of a school and the quality of its media program, although some principals of older schools shrug and say, "What can we do? We don't have room for a library." This is no excuse. There has to be room—on the stage, in the cafeteria, a corner of the hall, or in individual classrooms.

A school in Florida uses its stage to shelve its books and disperses its media equipment in small centers throughout the school. Another school with a large foyer near the office created a hall center by putting in indoor-outdoor carpeting, bookshelves, cupboards for media, and a few tables. Since the school is not on a rigid schedule where students pass through the halls on the hour, hall traffic does not interfere with class and student use of the center, and it is readily accessible when students are in the hall before and after school and at noon. If it's space you lack, look around and see what you can find.

◆ OPENING THE LIBRARY

"Opening the library" means the library is open for use, not only in the sense that children come and go through the doorway but that once inside they find books and equipment available to them.

The doors should open when the staff arrives in the morning and close when they go home at night. Encourage children to come in before school, after school, and during the noon hour. Although you may have to set limits, let individuals and small groups come in during the day, even though classes are scheduled.

Too many old schools have rules almost as old as the buildings. The rule, "Only one student out of a room at a time," or a policy that requires hall passes for children going to the lavatory, the library, or the drinking fountain are not consistent with an open library. With such rules, teachers spend time explaining why they can't give a pass, writing one out, or keeping track of a permanent one, and students spend their time plotting ways to get around the rules. A librarian can't concentrate on students and passes at the same time, so forget the passes. It may take a while to become accustomed to the idea, but students will assume the responsibility of going where they are supposed to go if given a chance.

Some librarians limit the number of students because they fear that heavy use of the library will result in chaos and confusion. If the library is empty, or almost so, of course it will be quiet, but when a number of students are engaged in learning activities, there will be some noise. Learning noise is different from goofing-off noise, and any teacher can tell the difference.

A child who is goofing off or disturbing others can be sent back to his classroom without fuss or fanfare. There are other ways to handle discipline problems, but practically speaking, if the library is to be open for student use, the librarian does not have time to worry about student behavior. When, through abuse, students temporarily lose their library privileges they learn that with freedom comes responsibility.

In some cases "open" might mean providing privacy through carrels; they are a must for students with learning disabilities and a help for those who are easily distracted.

Don't schedule the library in advance for long-term class use more than fifty per cent of the time. Post a weekly schedule in a prominent place, and let teachers sign up for open time each week. A flexible library schedule allows teachers more flexibility in their planning. We even encourage teachers to come on the spur of the moment but to check with the librarian first so two or three classes don't descend at the same time.

When teachers bring groups to the library, it is helpful if they, as well as the librarian, assist children in selecting and using materials. Bringing a class to the library is not a matter of "The librarian is in charge here, so I'll take it easy."

Some kind of in-service instruction in the use of library and media materials makes it easier for teachers to take an active part in the library program. They use the new media materials to advantage when they know more about them, and it is up to the librarian to help them learn.

Materials should be accessible to both teachers and students. Don't hide machines in cupboards. Put them out where people can see them and use them. Having to ask the librarian discourages use as does a complicated check-out system.

Arrange furniture and facilities for the comfort and convenience of the users. Children don't have to sit at tables. Have some tables, but also let the youngsters sprawl on the floor. They love pillows and beanbag chairs. Carpeting cuts down noise and makes the use of the floor more practical, but if carpeting is impossible, at least put down some small rugs. The object is to create a cozy, homelike atmosphere that makes children want to come in.

◆ CREATING MEDIA CENTERS

"I don't know what to do," a teacher complained. "These kids today are bored with everything. They don't listen. They have seen so much TV that I'd have to be Bugs Bunny or Captain Kangaroo to get their attention."

That teacher would rather change the kids than change his methods, but in one way he was right. TV has made a difference. Children today are informed and mature. They will learn by doing, but they won't sit still for lectures.

Different media, then, has to be utilized, and the media center is the means by which we improve instruction as we foster independent, self-directed learning. Children not only need books to read, they need machines to operate. It is as important for them to use machines to make their own tapes, film their own movies, and even produce their own film-strips as it is to learn from what has been prepared for them.

Most older libraries, however, were built to house only books. There is no room for the new media materials, but there are alternatives. Either expand the library space you have or disperse the materials.

When our school was built, it had no library. The library was added when new classrooms were added six years later, but as concepts changed and more and more media equipment became part of our library program, the space became inadequate. We expanded by removing the wall between the library and an adjoining classroom. Now we have room for media and room to accommodate a large class, individuals, and small groups at the same time.

But even if we hadn't been able to expand the library, we could still have had media centers. Media material does not need to be together in one central place. In fact, even if you have an adequate library center, it is a good idea to set up mini-media centers throughout the school to give children access to equipment for immediate use. Connect the centers to the main library through a central check-out system, so the librarian knows what is where. It is of no use to anyone if a picture set of American Indians, for example, is locked in one teacher's closet for ninety per cent of the school year.

You can have a center wherever you have children outside as well as inside the school building. A school in Gunnison, Colorado, puts tapes in its buses. An outdoor education laboratory would be another place for an effective center.

Requirements for classroom centers are the same as for library centers, only on a smaller scale. A small corner or space with one electrical outlet is all that is necessary. (One electric outlet is a minimum, but some older classrooms only have one. With an extension cord, two or three machines can be operated at the same time, but more might blow a circuit.)

Block off the area with a small bookcase, table, or screen,

put down a small rug, and set out the following supplies and equipment:

◇ Up to four sets of headphones.

◇ One filmstrip previewer or projector.

◇ A large piece of white paper for a screen or paint a white square on the wall.

◇ One record player.

◇ Books for reference and pleasure.

◇ Activities related to the curriculum.

◇ Additional games such as Quizmo, Name the State, or an electric board for multiplication facts.

The idea is to make the center cozy, comfortable, and convenient. Keep it interesting by changing materials periodically to relate to different subjects and units.

Children use a center to reinforce basic concepts, for exploratory purposes, and for follow-up activities. The following list suggests the kind of activity that can take place:

◇ Students listen to tapes or view filmstrips.

◇ Students explore through individual research.

◇ Students make their own filmstrips or slides. Scholastic sells an inexpensive kit that makes this easy to do.

◇ Students make 16mm movies. Film is relatively cheap, but the projector is expensive.

◇ Students use the cassette or tape recorder to prepare class presentations. They research their subjects, prepare visual materials such as slides, transparencies, filmstrips or murals, write scripts from research notes, and record them on cassettes. They bring in appropriate records for musical background and interest.

◇ Students make clay models, for example, a fish to go with a nature unit.

◇ Students make salt and flour maps and papier-mâché globes to go with map and globe units.

◇ Students use odds and ends such as bottle caps, string and ribbon, scraps of burlap, carpet and tiles, and foil or shiny paper for creative arts projects.

There is no limit to the possibilities for center activities. The students are sources of ideas, but setting up a successful center takes energy and imagination on the part of the teacher.

Rather than establish individual classroom centers, teachers on a team may share a center accessible to all of their students. This could be located in the hall, a small storeroom, or a classroom corner. Several classes then share an expensive piece of equipment. In either case, the librarian serves as a resource person to assist the classroom teacher.

♦ HOW TO INCREASE CIRCULATION

One cannot judge a school library by the amount of material in the library at any one time. On the contrary, there should be a constant flow of materials to and from the room. If at least half the materials are gone, it is a good sign that they are circulating.

It is up to the librarian to create a climate where the materials flow freely, but a positive and encouraging attitude toward books and reading prevailing throughout the school also affects circulation figures. To impress students with the importance of reading, some schools have initiated a special period called USSR (Uninterrupted, Sustained, Silent Reading) for half an hour a week or an hour every two weeks or fifteen minutes a day. At this time everyone in the school, including the custodian and the principal, reads something of his choice.

Books circulate more rapidly when the librarian is not overly concerned about a due back date. Collecting fines and harrassing children who fail to return a book on a specific date discourages check-out and wastes the librarian's time. They can even have a lasting effect. One old gentleman we know refuses to borrow books from the public library even though he has time on his hands. "I probably wouldn't get them back on time," he says, "and then there'd be trouble." This is an extreme example, but perhaps his lifetime reading habits were affected by an unpleasant school library experience.

Abolish the due date, and encourage children to take the number of books they will read within a reasonable period of time. When those books are returned, others may be checked out. Some will take two books at a time; others will take more. It is the child's responsibility to know his limit. If he has too many books out for too long a time, remind him, but don't harrass or embarrass him. To make it possible for children to keep a popular book for a longer period of time, we order up to five copies of books that are in demand.

One school thought that not enough books were circulating, so it passed out all the library books to the children in the school. Each child had about ten books that he was responsible for trading, and except for the original listing of who had what ten books, the librarian had no idea who had what. A child wanting a particular book, *Tom Sawyer* for instance, might have had to yell through the halls, "Who has *Tom Sawyer?*" to find it. Some books spent the year in a child's closet; others were lost in the shuffle. At the end of the year many books were missing. The system didn't work, and it wasn't repeated the next year.

There was some merit, however, in what the school was trying to do, even if its method was extreme. It was trying to get the books off the shelves and into the hands of readers, a concept foreign to too many school librarians. The authors of *Hooked On Books*, Daniel Fader and Elton McNeil, suggest giving each child a book or two at the beginning of the year. He trades with other students or the librarian, but the books are his to keep and to do with as he or she pleases.

Attractive bulletin boards and book and art displays will pique children's interest and encourage circulation. Children become tired of the same thing, so rotate the books you put out and keep bulletin boards up to date. Nothing gives children the idea that the librarian doesn't care like a back-to-school or early fall bulletin board still up on the last day of school. Aides and volunteers can take care of changing displays.

Because paperback book covers are bright and inviting, display them on racks where the covers show and put them within reach of children wanting to thumb through the ones that appeal to them. Book jackets, too, are designed to appeal to readers, so use them to whet students' curiosity.

National Library Week inspired a "Swing Into Spring" bulletin board theme in our library. First graders put a raindrop on the bulletin board for each book they read under the heading "Every Book Is a Drop of Knowledge." Second graders put a bug in the garden above the shelves, and third graders added flowers. Fourth-grade students put pink blossoms on a real branch, and a sign behind their display read "Blossom Out In Knowledge." Fifth and sixth graders completed the mural on an end wall with music notes and bars. The children loved to put up their symbols, and circulation figures climbed during this week.

At one time we had a library mascot, an owl chosen by the children, who did his best to encourage children to read. There were owl signs around such as "Old professor owl is a wise old owl, and he keeps things hooting around here." A rubber stamp made in the mascot's likeness was used on notes written by the librarian or the teacher to motivate children to read a particular book, give approval for a job well done, point out rules, and to urge them to treat books and materials as they would a best friend. If a child had a book out for a long period of time, the owl might ask him about it. Children liked the idea and usually responded to the owl's suggestions.

Student projects such as shadow boxes that depict stories available in the library make others want to read those stories. Student art displays recognize those who have done the creative work besides lending interest to library walls and shelves.

Reproductions of art masterpieces, either purchased or on loan, bring famous people, legends, and myths to life for children. Ask the parent organization to purchase several prints and pieces of sculpture over a period of time to build up a library collection. Then set up trades with other schools during the school year to extend your collection even farther.

◆ USING OUTSIDE LIBRARY SOURCES TO INCREASE RESOURCES

A new library and media center is seldom able to acquire all the books, pictures, filmstrips, tapes, and other media desired. In fact, seldom is any library well enough equipped to satisfy the needs of all students. It is necessary, therefore, to look to outside sources.

Some districts work with other school districts to organize boards of cooperative services with a central media center. This saves each district money because one or two people coordinate exchanges and the schools obtain more material for less money. Among other things the center processes books, lends films, coordinates picture set and learning kit exchanges, and maintains a professional library.

Book exchanges with the local library, book and media exchanges with schools in the district, and visits from a traveling bookmobile can all increase the resources of the school library.

❖❖❖❖❖❖❖❖❖❖❖❖❖❖❖❖❖❖❖❖❖❖❖❖❖

PROVIDING FOR CHILDREN
WITH
LEARNING DISABILITIES

"When the Diamonds Don't Touch"
❖❖❖❖❖

A THIRD-GRADE TEACHER NOTICED THAT A CHILD IN HER CLASS
was having trouble cutting with scissors, holding her pencil,
and forming her letters. The teacher mentioned these observations to the school psychologist who, with parent permission, gave the child a diagnostic test. A picture on the
test showed two diamonds touching. As part of the test,
the child was asked to reproduce the picture. She drew the
diamonds an inch and a half apart. She drew the diamonds
as she perceived them, and she perceived them this way
because she had a learning disability.*

Although many children have a learning disability,
approximately one child in twenty is affected to the extent
that he does not benefit from regular classroom instruction,
and it is this child who needs special help.

We are not referring to children with some other major
handicap, such as blindness or deafness, or the mentally
retarded or the emotionally disturbed. We are speaking of
children, usually of average intelligence, who are per-

---

* A psychological test will indicate the possible presence of a learning
disability, but to identify the specific disability, an educational specialist needs to do an educational evaluation.

ceptually or conceptually handicapped. For some neurological reason, they have an impediment in understanding, in reception, organization, or expression of the written or spoken language. Because of their handicap, they are unable to respond to the usual classroom methods and procedures. Listening, reading, writing, and any other work with symbols pose particular problems for these children.

Imagine how frustrating it must be for a child who cannot learn the same way other children do. If the teacher doesn't understand, she thinks he is dumb or lazy, and soon the other children do too, while in reality, he is trying but is not able to do what is expected of him. It is not suprising then that he finally gives up and turns to doing whatever he can do, even if it is just causing trouble. Recent studies, in fact, show that a high percentage of children who have been arrested for one reason or another have a learning disability.

The problem is not new. Ever since there has been formal education, there have been children with learning disabilities. Although many people have succeeded in spite of a learning disability because they learned on their own to compensate for their problems, many, many more have failed in school and in life.

What is new is that schools are now recognizing these problems and are trying to do something about them. This includes identifying children with disabilities, devising ways to help those with minor problems in the classrooms, and establishing a special program for those who need more help. The goal of the special program is to return the child to his regular classroom as soon as he is able to function satisfactorily there.

In some cases, due to court rulings and legislative actions, schools no longer have a choice as to whether or not to implement a program. They are either required by law or prodded through monetary incentives to establish special classes for the learning disabled.

◆ IDENTIFYING CHILDREN WITH LEARNING DISABILITIES

The sooner a learning disability is identified, the better it is for the child. With proper training he can learn to compensate for his disability, but he should have the training before he gets behind academically and his self-concept suffers. Once he sees himself as dumb, the image is hard to change.

Regardless of whether the school has a program, classroom teachers should be familiar with learning disability symptoms. If there is no professional help available in the school, the classroom teacher can refer the child and his parents to people or programs, such as a physician or a college or university clinic that can do something for him. If there is an in-school teacher or class, the first referral usually comes from the classroom teacher anyway.

Although most classroom teachers aren't trained to diagnose specific learning disabilities, if a child displays the following symptoms with frequency and consistency, and if it has been determined that he is of normal intelligence, the teacher should refer him to someone who can do further testing.

◇ His general classroom behavior is inconsistent and erratic.

◇ His classroom functioning and production are not commensurate with his apparent ability.

◇ His emotional reactions are inappropriate to the occasion.

◇ He either talks too much or too little.

◇ He is either too aggressive or too passive.

◇ He has difficulty changing from one task to another.

◇ He lacks concentration on a given task.

◇ He lacks coordination in activities involving use of his gross and/or fine muscles.

◇   He is generally awkward and clumsy.

◇   He has trouble following either written or oral directions.

◇   He has a short attention span.

◇   He is easily distracted.

◇   Frequently he does not complete a task.

◇   He has trouble getting along with adults and/or his peers.

◇   He possesses identifiable perceptual difficulties, i.e., copy-
     ing from the board, mirror writing, visual or auditory
     discrimination, directionality, or visual or auditory reversals.

◇   He shows excessive inconsistency in his quality or per-
     formance from day to day, hour to hour.

◇   He is impulsive.

◇   His speech is immature for his age.

◇   He says or does the same thing over and over.

If a child displays a few of these symptoms occasionally,
it does not mean he has a learning disability. *Frequency*
and *consistency* are the key words.

Once a teacher thinks he has identified a child with a
learning disability, he needs to write out some kind of a
referral. The referral form on the opposite page includes
program definition and purpose.

Even though a teacher may not know how to correct a
specific learning disability, knowing what learning disabilities are and understanding that a child has one helps,
because a teacher who thinks a child is dumb, communicates
that attitude to the entire class.

◆ ESTABLISHING A PROGRAM WITHIN
   THE SCHOOL

A team approach, even in the planning stages, produces
more cooperation and understanding throughout the school
once a learning disability program is under way. Begin by
forming a team composed of a teacher certified in special

SCHOOL REFERRAL FOR CONSIDERATION FOR EDUCATIONALLY HANDICAPPED PROGRAM

SCHOOL_____TEACHER(S)_____

CHILD'S NAME_____SEX_____AGE_____

PARENT'S NAME_____TELEPHONE_____

ADDRESS_____

PRINCIPAL'S SIGNATURE_____DATE_____

1. DEFINITION

An educationally handicapped child refers to one who is not receiving the full benefit of the regular classroom educational opportunities because he usually has difficulty in learning the use of symbolic language and abstract material. He may be characterized by such descriptions as distractible, hyperactive, impulsive and inconsistent in his ability to learn and retain facts and skills. These characteristics have contributed to a learning developmental lag.

2. PURPOSE OF THE PROGRAM

With individualized instruction by a specifically prepared teacher and in a small group the child has the opportunity to learn to compensate for his specific learning disability. The goal is to provide growth opportunity so he can function satisfactorily in his regular school setting.

3. Please check the following characteristics which describe the student:

___He knows what he wants to say but cannot say it.

___He may learn something one day but seems to have completely forgotten it the next day.

___He misses a total concept because he often cannot figure out what is going on around him.

___He really tries but easily becomes frustrated.

___He is easily distracted because all items have equal value to him and he can't concentrate on any one thing.

___He needs a structured, but not rigid, environment.

___He appears to react without thinking and often demands immediate attention.

4. Describe briefly and concisely the child's classroom behavior which has elicited your concern_____

_____

_____

5. Specific learning problems_____

_____

_____

education—called an educational specialist—the school counselor, unit leaders, a school or district psychologist, and the school principal. Decide on a program definition and purpose to fit the needs of your school and your students and work from there. As you plan, seek advice from special consultants, the state department of education, or outside school personnel who have had experience with programs of their own.

The same team establishes criteria for admission into the program. Because of other overriding problems, some children wouldn't benefit from a learning disability program, and although many students have learning disabilities, no school has enough money or trained personnel to work with each of them in a special class. Perhaps as classroom teachers receive more training in this area, they will be able to help children with minor problems in their own classrooms. Meantime, selections must be made.

Our team developed the following criteria for admission into our program:

◇ Intelligence. The child must be capable of normal intelligence.

◇ Physical status. The child must not be affected by a gross physical disability such as blindness or deafness.

◇ Identified deficit. The learning deficit must be specific. The deficits may be in the areas of eye-hand coordination, spacial relationships, general muscular coordination, or other, such as a weakness in auditory or visual method.

◇ Diagnosis of difficulty should indicate minimal emotional disturbance.

The team, with the child's homeroom teacher taking the place of the unit leaders, serves as a selection committee, and once a child is admitted to the program, they work together to correct his problem.

Each child is affected differently, so his individual problem must be dealt with differently by a teacher trained to correct it; yet one of our objectives is to maintain the child in the regular classroom environment during most of the school day. Children don't like to be singled out or be made to feel different from their classmates, and although many children with learning disabilities need a more structured approach to their studies than the regular school program provides, it is not wise to isolate them.

You can establish a headquarters classroom where children with learning disabilities work with a special teacher part of the time and with their own class the rest of the day. Older children sometimes prefer not to go to a special learning station. In this case the special teacher works with the child in the regular classroom. In either case cooperation between the classroom teacher and the special teacher is essential.

Regular teachers often find it hard to believe that it takes a special teacher to teach a bright child in their classroom to read. Some classroom teachers resent a special teacher taking a child out of the classroom part of the day, and some special teachers don't make enough effort to explain their program to the classroom teacher. The team approach helps, but it does take understanding on both sides to make the program succeed.

Several teachers in the school, in addition to the special learning disabilities teacher, may be responsible for the child. Perhaps he works with a speech therapist or has a P.E. teacher different from his homeroom teacher. If so, the special teacher needs to meet with the teacher to plan his weekly program and to talk about expectations for him in the special class and in the regular class.

Team cooperation, in one instance, centered around a child who had some motor coordination deficits. The P.E. teacher observed, and the other teachers agreed, that the child's self-esteem needed boosting when he played a playground game with his peers that involved underhanded throwing. The special teacher helped the child develop better coordination by using a beanbag toss game. This technically is called skill transfer—learning a skill and transferring it to other situations. His skill did improve and so did his self-esteem.

The same method works for the child having difficulty learning work attack skills. The special teacher works with the child, teaching him to compensate for his deficit, and the classroom teachers reinforce the skill in the regular reading class.

By encouraging classroom teachers to take courses in the field of learning disabilities and by providing in-service activities in the area, principals can improve the learning disability program and increase the number of children who can be helped. The special teacher's assistance in planning in-service programs is valuable. Plan around various teacher groupings. For example, at the beginning of the school year, discuss the learning disability program in general with new teachers or teachers new to the school. Later plan a program to teach teachers specific ways to teach handwriting to children who are plagued with reversals, or how to teach left-to-right sequencing to children who have a problem with that.

In-service programs and parent counseling are a part of the total learning disability program. Parents as well as teachers need to understand that these children don't learn in the usual way, not because they don't want to, but because they can't. Actively soliciting parent volunteer aid is a way to get parents into the classroom where they can see firsthand how the class operates and how their child is progressing within it.

The special teacher evaluates the child's progress during his tenure in the class according to methods determined by the child's team. These may include parent conferences, written description of student progress, informal teacher-made tests, and more formal tests issued by various publishers. When the child achieves the goals his team has set for him, he graduates from the program, and that means he returns full-time to the regular classroom. We found that some children were dependent and still clung to the special teacher even after they returned to their regular class, so we use the word "graduated" because it has a final connotation and discourages dependency.

One child who had many problems seemed to prove the success of the program when, after he had graduated and returned to his regular class, the special teacher asked him what he did during his reading class, and he said matter-of-factly, "Why, I do what everybody else does!"

◆ ORGANIZING A CENTER FOR CHILDREN WITH LEARNING DISABILITIES

When it comes to providing facilities for a learning disability program, old schools are on an equal footing with new ones. It is difficult to work on specific strengths and weaknesses of individual students in a large open area, so even some new schools still in the planning stage are including a closed area for a learning disability program.

The center requires many different pieces of equipment. Children will be working with record players, tape recorders, filmstrip viewers, a balance beam, games and puzzles, or even a typewriter. Therefore, you need a room with sufficient electrical outlets and large enough to house and operate the different machines.

Our learning disability room had a small storeroom next to a classroom. The teacher cleared it out and put in a desk so students could have privacy. For example, they can read a story into a tape recorder without being self-conscious about it. Carrels in the classroom can perform the same purpose.

The teacher also used a shelf divider to set off a small carpeted area. The children stretched out in the area to work with matching cards or some such project. Sometimes they hid behind the shelves to avoid being "found out" by others when they were working on something simple, such as addition facts.

There are not more than three or four children in the

room at the same time because they rotate to their regular classrooms, but they do need room to work at different stations. A room of classroom size is not too large if you can spare the space.

This program should not be jammed into a closet or small planning room. If this is all you have to offer, it would be better to have the educational specialist serve as a resource person who works with teachers and individual children in their classrooms rather than trying to establish a separate learning disability classroom program.

◆ ALTERNATIVE PROGRAMS

Some schools are either too small or their budget limitations too great to employ a full-time educational specialist. One of the following alternative programs might work for these schools.

A teacher shared by several school districts or several schools within the same district visits the schools weekly or biweekly. He is called a visiting teacher, floating specialist, or itinerant teacher.

He diagnoses student problems and works out learning prescriptions. He shows teachers how and what materials to use, and he periodically evaluates the child's progress. He won't know the child as well as if he were stationed in the school, and he might not have the time to consult with the child's other teachers, but he can help the child overcome a specific disability.

Another possibility, although not as effective as using a thoroughly trained teacher, is to select a classroom teacher, preferably one who has already shown some interest in learning disabilities, to serve as a resource person for the school. Encourage this individual, through released time, to attend workshops or classes on the subject and then allow some time in his schedule for him to work with the learning disabled.

Tutorial programs have proved successful in some areas,

usually where there is a college or university training program. College students or parents are trained to work with the learning disabled through a volunteer program, or there could be compensation. However, not just anybody is equipped to work with the learning disabled, no matter how willing he may be, so if there is no nearby training program and a classroom teacher has had some training, reverse the tutor role. Have the college student or parent volunteer take over the large classroom group for a time while the classroom teacher tutors the children with learning disabilities.

Pennsylvania State University has a new concept that it calls an assessment class. It has a mobile unit staffed by two master teachers that moves to different schools and focuses on approximately five children over a six-week period. The teachers work primarily with younger children, and their object is to condition them for regular schooling.

INCORPORATING
OUTDOOR EDUCATION

"Down to Earth Experiences"
❖❖❖❖❖

TODAY MOST CHILDREN LIVE IN CITIES AND SUBURBS. THEY ARE surrounded by brick and concrete, and there is little left of a natural environment. They breathe polluted air, they see billboards, junk yards, and litter. They hear of water pollution and vanishing wildlife species.

Teaching these children the three R's is no longer enough. Unless we add outdoor education and a fourth R—resources—to the curriculum, we may find that sometime in the future, we won't have the materials such as pencils and papers with which to practice the other three.

Outdoor education can teach conservation of the natural resources necessary for man's survival on this planet. It can help students understand their environment, what it is, how it changed, and the interdependence of all living things. It can teach problem-solving through life experience.

Hopefully, outdoor education will involve hearts as well as heads. Recently in our area, giant cottonwood trees over a hundred years old growing along a canal were cut and destroyed for no apparent reason other than an urge to destroy. Newspaper stories tell of vandals who dig up park plantings or who cut their Christmas tree in someone's yard. Perhaps those who perform such destructive acts have never planted a tree or watched a seed sprout. We talk of teaching values and attitudes such as responsibility and self-reliance. What better way to do this than having students learn from nature instead of about her?

◆ ESTABLISHING AN OUTDOOR LEARNING LABORATORY

An outdoor learning laboratory on the school grounds is one way to incorporate outdoor education into the school program. New schools can include a laboratory in their planning, but if you have an old school, where do you put it? Take a creative look at your school grounds. Perhaps you can spare a corner of the playground, part of a parking lot (concrete and blacktop aren't sacred), a center courtyard, a parkway area between the sidewalk and the street, or a foot or two running along a fence. One teacher found a few square feet of dirt beneath a fire escape. If there is absolutely no other space, window boxes or planters are better than nothing at all.

Sometimes problem areas, those too hilly or too wet or otherwise undesirable, are ideal for an outdoor learning laboratory. We had a hill behind the school building, adjacent to the playground and the parking lot. It was not practical for playground use, and it was hard to supervise. We did plant crested wheat grass, but there were more weeds than grass, and the hill did nothing to improve the appearance of the school. When we surveyed our site, looking for a place to put our outdoor learning laboratory, we decided on that hill. Trees and plants and picnic tables have turned it into an asset rather than a liability.

Space isn't the only problem. An outdoor project costs money. We are fortunate in that our district allots each school so much a year for landscaping. When we decided to go ahead with an outdoor laboratory, we started with this allowance.

If you have no money in the budget, there are several ways to obtain financial help. The PTA might undertake the lab as its yearly project and raise funds to support it. Class gifts, federal funds, and industrial grants are all possibilities. Community service organizations such as the Lions or Kiwanis Clubs might help.

Students can help organize and participate in fund raising projects. Projects having to do with ecology, such as collecting and selling recyclable materials, not only help finance the laboratory but give students the satisfaction of knowing they are saving natural resources and helping solve the waste disposal problem.

Irving Elementary School in Pueblo, Colorado, received a $750 grant from the Chevron Oil Company, a $300 donation from the Pueblo Lions Club, and the students earned $200 by collecting material for recycling to start their outdoor laboratory.

A worthwhile project seems to attract donations, and it seems once you have a project and a plan, you can find ways to complete it. For instance, we usually purchased a Christmas tree for the school with money from the school fund. The year we started our laboratory the staff decided to spend the money we usually spent for a Christmas tree, which stood in the hall for a couple of weeks and was thrown out with the trash, for a four and a half-foot live pinion pine to be planted in the laboratory. Our counselor donated an aluminum tree for the hall. Since then, a live tree for the laboratory has become our Christmas tradition.

◆ DEVELOP A PLAN

In our school district, decisions such as to establish an outdoor learning laboratory are left to the school principal, but in many districts a proposal would have to be submitted to the school board. A resource specialist, landscape architect, or soil conservation person can help with the proposal. In preparing a presentation, goals and benefits must be clearly stated.

Although we did not present a proposal to the board, we

did write out a statement of purpose for our own use. The statement, based on an outdoor learning center proposal written by Dr. James Camaren, follows:

> Education in the outdoor learning laboratory will be partially based on the premise that "learning can be fun." Emphasis will be placed upon teaching the *whole* child; that is, concern for him as an individual as well as for his academic achievement.
>
> *Learning Through Direct Experiences.* The laboratory will not only be a place where a child gains knowledge, it will provide him with opportunities to apply that knowledge through problem-solving experiences. He will learn by doing.
>
> *Motivation for Learning.* It is anticipated that the outdoor laboratory will provide new opportunities for student motivation and success. Those who aren't motivated and do not succeed in a regular classroom often achieve in a natural, informal, outdoor setting.
>
> *Utilization of All the Senses.* Outdoor learning through direct experience will involve all of the senses. Research shows that retention of knowledge in such circumstances tends to be long-lasting.
>
> *Stimulation of Creative Ability.* There will be opportunities in this classroom outside the classroom to develop creative talent in all children, regardless of their academic levels.
>
> *Appreciation of Natural Resources.* Through the laboratory, children will learn the value of their natural heritage. They will learn of man's dependence upon natural resources for survival, and they will become concerned about the conservation of those resources.
>
> *Understanding Man's Relation to His Environment.* Students will see, through actual life experiences, how man's decisions affect other living things. They will better understand the interdependence of all life.
>
> *Development of Social Skills.* The laboratory will provide opportunities for children to work together in a cooperative venture. They will learn to do their part and cooperate with others if projects are to be successful.

The next step, after goals have been determined and the project has been approved, is to inventory the school site.

According to a Department of Agriculture publication, *Outdoor Classrooms on School Sites*, you will be looking for:

◇ Vegetation—grasses, shrubs, trees, weeds, wildflowers, plants harmful to people such as poison ivy and nettles, and vegetation in old fields for studies of plant succession.

◇ Topographic and geologic features—rock outcrops, boulders, slopes, streams, ponds, and wet areas.

◇ Animal habitats—den and nesting trees, brush piles, food plants, old stumps, and fallen logs.

◇ Soil profiles exposed on banks and slopes, potential soil erosion, and soil study areas.

◇ Historical remnants such as old stone fences and orchards.

◇ Sites that would be appropriate for learning trails with study areas and listening posts.

When you know what you have to work with, work out a plan so development will be orderly. The plan should be long range, providing for additions and improvements in the years to come. It is wise to form a committee to guide the development. Our committee is composed of parents, teachers, students, the principal, and the landscape architect.

As your committee plans, certain questions will need to be answered. Are water, electricity, or natural gas available? Should the area be fenced to prevent unauthorized use? Who will be responsible for maintaining the laboratory during the summer vacation period? Is it desirable to include a greenhouse? Will there be a place for picnic tables? What about raising rabbits, pheasants, or other animals? Is a small pond desirable?

Once these and other questions have been answered, you are ready to proceed.

Involve the students and the school community. The more they work on and for the laboratory, the greater their pride and sense of accomplishment will be.

When we planted our Christmas pinion pine, the first planting in the laboratory, the whole school turned out to watch the ceremony. A representative from each class turned a shovelful of dirt. Four sixth graders, one from each sixth-grade class, prepared statements that they read as they dedicated the area. It was a quiet and solemn occasion. The students were told that as they grew, the trees and plants in the area would grow, and someday they might come back and see what they had begun. They were there at the beginning, and they were involved.

Students can care for plants, mark trails, pull weeds, find specimens, and supervise younger students. Although large trees will have to be handled by professionals, the students themselves can do most other planting. Students, as we suggested earlier, can participate in fund raising projects. They can help decide how the money is to be spent.

Your outdoor laboratory need not concern only school children during school hours. Involve the adult community too. They can learn from the laboratory, and they will feel that they have a part in it if they do something to help. One city school had a Saturday "plant in." A father who owned a tractor drove it to the school and plowed the area. Families worked together to plant shrubs, trees, vines, and flowers. This same school asked families to donate bricks for a path that would meander through the laboratory. They donated what they could, three or four bricks or several hundred, and the path was completed. Vandalisı ı has not been a problem here, perhaps because the entire community is involved.

Involve community youth organizations too, such as the Scouts or the Camp Fire Girls. You will need someone to water and maintain the laboratory over the summer months, and Scouts or Camp Fire Girls can earn merit badges by taking care of it.

◆ USE IMAGINATION AND INGENUITY TO DEVELOP A SMALL SITE

Every laboratory should be unique, tailored to fit a particular school, a particular community, a particular climate, and a particular site. What you do with a forty-acre site in New Mexico will be entirely different from what you do with a concrete-covered, city site. Here are some ideas for a small site:

◇ If you are working with minimum space, you will have to make the most of what you have. A study of ecology might start with a crack in a sidewalk. Supply students with cheap magnifying glasses and let them study insect and plant life around the crack. Help them find out why the concrete cracked in the first place.

◇ Wherever you find a few feet of soil, plant trees, shrubs, grasses, and flowers native to your area.

◇ Fence an anthill on the grounds and study the ants.

◇ Mount birdhouses and feeders on the grounds or next to the building.

◇ A glass beehive located in a corner of a greenhouse or in a corner of the school grounds is another possibility.

◇ Greenhouses built onto or next to the school building occupy little space. They make it possible for students in areas with limited grounds or a limited growing season to study plant propagation by seed, cuttings, and grafting, and to grow their own fruits and vegetables. Greenhouses range from expensive manufactured models to plastic and wood-frame student-teacher constructions.

◇ Few school grounds are too small for a sundial. Use a half circle of concrete and an old pipe to help students understand the movement of the sun and the change of seasons.

◇ Fertilizer experiments can be done with beans in cans or on small sections of grass sod. Students find out what fertilizers plants need and how plants react to fertilization.

◇ Using a soil thermometer, students can take soil temperatures near the building, under a tree, and in the center of the school ground every day for several months. Then they can graph figures they compiled to show the differences.

The preceding suggestions should get you started, but don't be limited by them. Perhaps you can apply some of the suggestions in the next section to your laboratory, only on a smaller scale. You, your students, and your resource specialist will come up with other ideas. Remember, you are limited only by your imagination.

◆ LARGE SITE PROJECTS TO BE PLANNED BY AND FOR STUDENTS

If you have a medium to large site, you are fortunate because you have more options. You can incorporate the small site suggestions as well as large site projects into your overall plan. Adapt any of the following large site projects suggested to fit your needs:

◇ Make trails through the area with sawdust, wood chips, gravel, or brick.

◇ Make signs identifying plantings or exhibits. These may be made from boards or half logs with the words painted or burned on with a wood-burning tool. Some schools put numbers by the exhibits, and students make maps with an identification key.

◇ Make a soil pit to study the soil profile. One side should be vertical so students can see top soil and sub soil. Spray it with airplane glue to hold it in place. Provide a shelter over the hole to protect it from the rain. This could be a soil center where students study top soil, organic matter, soil texture, and weathering processes. Models could show contour farming, stubble-mulching, raindrop splash, and plant cover.

◇ Some areas have natural ponds, but if yours does not, you can make a small pond, about 10 x 12 feet and 2 feet deep, by lining a hole with plastic. Plant water lilies, cattails, sedges, and bullrushes in soil boxes and set the boxes in the shallow water. Ponds make it possible to study goldfish, frogs, tadpoles, water weeds, moss, and plankton.

◇ Students can research trees, shrubs, and grasses native to the area and devote an area to native plantings.

◇ Make a compost pit to demonstrate recycling of wastes. Use garbage from the lunchroom.

◇ Include a sundial, evaporation pans, maximum-minimum

thermometer, rain gauges, snow measuring platforms, wind direction, and velocity meters in a weather study area.

◇ By burning a small patch of land, students learn how plants and grasses restore themselves. Most states have air pollution laws, so obtain permission from the proper authorities. Also notify the fire department. It might want to stand by.

◇ Picnic tables provide a place for rest, class instruction, or lunch.

◇ A pile of undisturbed soil with stakes in it can be used to measure soil erosion. Another method is to put a nail through a washer and see how the soil erodes around it.

◇ Display a collection of rocks and minerals found in your area along a geological path. Some schools embed the rocks in concrete.

◇ If you have a slope, make terraces of old railroad ties to hold the soil in place and prevent erosion. Plant grasses, shrubs, and ground cover on the terrace.

◆ WHERE TO OBTAIN INFORMATION ON CONSERVATION ACTIVITIES

The Soil Conservation Service, Extension Service, and Forest Service of the U.S. Department of Agriculture are among the federal agencies that can assist in developing outdoor classrooms. These agencies have regional, state, or local offices. Telephone directories list these offices under "United States Government."

Many national and state conservation organizations, industrial associations, and citizens groups have local chapters or units that will help with conservation projects. *The Conservation Directory* (152 pages, $1.50), revised and published annually by the National Wildlife Federation, Washington, D.C., lists many of these organizations.

◆ LEARNING FROM FIELD TRIPS

While a miniature area on a city school ground may serve as an outdoor laboratory, it may not be large enough to meet the needs of the school population. To enlarge your outdoor education program, extend it beyond the school grounds through field trips.

If buses are available, bus students to parks or recreation areas; if they are not, use the immediate area in whatever way you can. If there is a park nearby, walk to it. Even if there is nothing in sight but concrete and pavement, take the children into the community to observe the social life, the architecture, and the service shops.

Field trips offer opportunities for high school students to work with younger students under a teacher's supervision. In one school district the teachers planned mini-walks where, over a period of months, high school students took elementary students on study tours. They took short fifteen to twenty minute walks around the school and through the community. Classroom studies coincided with the outdoor observations, and changes that took place with the changing seasons were noted and recorded.

The discovery of a beehive led one group to trace worker bees as they gathered pollen. Another group observed activity near and around the beehive (from a safe distance, of course). Others studied pond life in a nearby pool of water, while a fourth group studied and graphed ground temperature near buildings, under trees, and in the open with the aid of a ground thermometer. The high school students admitted, when the program was over, that they had learned as much or more than the elementary students.

It is easier to integrate younger and older students from the same building when they go outside where they have room to be together. In a district where buses were available for field trips, two teachers planned a trip where sixth graders teamed up with kindergartners to visit the site of a rock-fill dam that had been partially washed away by a flood years before. With the teachers' help the sixth graders scouted the area and planned the day's activities. They decided to divide the classes into interest groups with each kindergartner and his "buddy" spending the morning concentrating on one activity.

The "Compass Walk" group plotted their walk with compass and tape measure and laid out directions like a treasure hunt. Then the sixth graders helped the kindergartners use a compass and measure "30 feet to the ponderosa pine with the red X." The "Ecology and Plant" group studied the habitat and interaction between living and nonliving things. They cast plaster molds of animal prints that they found. The "Geology Party" hiked along rock formations and talked about the geology of the area. The "Dam" group discussed what a plaque told them of the history of the dam. The "Photographers" divided among the other activity groups and photographed the high spots of the trip.

Later back at school each group reported to the others, and they put it all together. Both age groups gained from the shared experience, socially as well as academically.

Every community has something to offer, and outdoor education does not have to mean nature. Use the resources available to you to make children aware of the world around them and to help them relate to it.

PROMOTING INTER-CULTURAL EXPERIENCES

"You Won't Have Any Trouble Recognizing Him"
❖❖❖❖

RECENTLY OUR STUDENTS SAW THE PUPPET SHOW *Stars and Stripes*. It concerned two characters, one covered with stars and the other covered with stripes, who were friends until they discovered that they looked different. The discovery affected their friendship. They became enemies and built a wall between themselves. After several battles, the two puppets found they were connected to the same person. What hurt one, hurt the other. Realizing then that even though they looked different they were part of the same person, they became friends once more.

Children in many school communities have little opportunity to discover that people outside their community are more like them than they are different. This lack is more evident in a suburban area than in a city-centered school community. Track houses built at the same time to sell at the same price house people of the same economic level with much the same background. Children in a community such as ours may never have met a child who can't afford to buy his lunch. They seldom meet a person of another race or nationality. This was particularly apparent when a black family enrolled, and we asked the mother the child's name. As she was talking with us the father was watching our students. "I don't think you'll have any trouble recognizing him," he commented.

Because people are more mobile than they used to be, children don't see grandparents as much as they used to. Very few older people live in suburban neighborhoods, so suburban children don't have a chance to relate to this age group either.

Academic experience alone will not equip children for today's world. They are deprived when all they know about other people is confined to their neighborhood experience. Without added expense the schools can actively promote outside contact. Possibilities include hiring teachers of different races and cultures, cultural awareness programs, exchange programs, and bringing in community people to share hobbies and interests.

The age of a school or its design has little to do with cultural experiences that faculty and administration can plan for children. It is people who make the difference whether or not children learn compassion for and understanding of others. It is as necessary to promote meaningful inter-cultural experiences in a closed school as in an open school, and in the central city as in the suburbs. As in *Stars and Stripes*, when people discover they are part of a whole, the walls come down.

◆ HIRING STAFF WITH VARIOUS CULTURAL AND RACIAL BACKGROUNDS

A faculty composed of teachers and paraprofessionals of varying cultural and racial backgrounds does more to teach understanding than any proclamation of "thou shalt." Every-day contact leads to knowing people as individuals rather than as a race, a religion, or a nationality. The more varied the backgrounds, the more educational possibilities are present.

A teacher in our school from West Pakistan, for example, brings something of her country to the children belonging to our third-grade team. They see the art, taste the food, model the saris, learn the dances, and hear of the customs. Thus the Pakistani culture becomes real for them.

A conscious effort to hire for diversity rather than sameness will help further cultural awareness goals in a way that study without related life experience never can.

◆ PROVIDING MEANINGFUL CULTURAL AWARENESS PROGRAMS

The faculty of Dry Creek Elementary School in our district recognized a need to break the cultural barriers surrounding the school community and instituted a program designed to develop an awareness of the contributions of the various cultures to American life. Their program has three basic purposes:

1. To provide the vehicle for improved self-concept, cultural understanding, and human relations.

2. To give children an opportunity to extend their learning and appreciation of the fine arts.

3. To afford an academic adventure in geography, history, customs, and peoples of other lands.

The program uses the area of the fine arts to explore different cultures for two reasons: *(1)* all cultures past and present are reflected in their arts, and *(2)* fine arts lend themselves to action-oriented projects, which are essential when working with elementary-aged children.

The program is composed of three interrelated parts. First the boys and girls are taken into the cultural and fine arts environment of the metropolitan area to visit cultural and fine arts performances and places.

The second part comes to the children. Individuals or performing groups are invited to the school to give a demonstration or performance in a face-to-face situation. This provides experiences that enrich the pupils' appreciation of the art forms, but above all, the people serve as models of the culture they represent.

During the third phase the children are divided into small groups in which they actively participate in art, drama, dance, and musical activities that relate to the culture they are studying. Studies become more meaningful as they learn by doing.

The faculty hopes that through studying people of other cultures the children will gain a better understanding of themselves and their place in society and, consequently, will develop open minds and tolerant attitudes to prepare them to live harmoniously in a multi-ethnic society.

Two teachers and one teacher's aide have the primary responsibility for the program. They plan units for four-week blocks of time with groups of twenty to thirty children scheduled to participate at specific times during the day.

The four-week unit on the Spanish-speaking culture, for example, includes speakers who show slides and films about the culture, Mexican and Spanish art projects, and lessons in Mexican folk dancing. Field trips take children into Spanish communities, and some student visitation exchanges are arranged. Bulletin boards display the art work, written reports, newspaper articles, and pertinent notices that have to do with the unit.

Scheduled events from different units have included speakers whose topics were "The Black Man in Western History" and "The Spanish-Speaking Culture Today," a field trip to a local theatre to see *Sounder*, a trip to a Jewish synagogue, and a Kabuki make-up demonstration.

◆ EXCHANGE PROGRAMS WITH OTHER SCHOOLS

Student exchange programs offer still another way for children to learn first-hand about life styles in other communities. One school faculty plans a six-week study unit with an exchange school faculty that is climaxed with a one-day student exchange. The unit includes activities that help students understand cultural differences that exist. For example, the groups write letters to each other telling of their respective schools and communities. In addition to what they gain from the exchange of information, they put to use what they have learned about grammar, punctuation, penmanship, paragraphing, and descriptive writing. They draw or paint pictures of their schools and their homes. The art projects are also exchanged in advance of the visits.

The day of the exchange half the students and faculty of each school go to the other school to visit, and half stay at the home school. Visiting students read, write, and take part in math lessons just as if they were regular students of the school. The teachers, of course, do try to plan lessons for the day with the visitors in mind. In addition to participating in classroom activities, students talk to children their own age and observe life in the other school. Follow-up activities include thank-you notes, discussions, and written impressions.

Two other schools exchanged visits shortly before Christmas. A group of sixty first-grade suburban children invited inner-city school first-grade children, most of whom were black, to their Christmas program. The visitors then gave a program in return. Both groups were basically of the same economic level, and it is interesting to note that the children were surprised to find that they had much in common. They were overheard to comment, "He likes what I like," "She dresses like I do," and "He taught me how to play a new game."

Schools not close to a city can still have exchange programs, and because they do not have as much contact with outside communities, perhaps it is even more important for them to do so. In one such case, suburban children exchanged with children from a school located in an Indian reservation. The suburban children traveled by bus and spent several days at the school. They slept in the school gymnasium and ate in the school and in the nearby town.

The chaperons were the only ones who complained of sore backs after two nights in a sleeping bag on the gym floor. When the Indian children returned the visit, they each stayed with a "buddy" and his family.

◆ UTILIZING COMMUNITY RESOURCE PEOPLE

A community resource program can provide exciting inter-cultural experiences for children as well as enrich the school curriculum. The term "utilizing community resource people" means identifying people living in the community who are willing to share their knowledge, expertise, and experience with children and organizing them as an integral part of the school's instructional program. The purpose of the program is to assist the teachers by using the community as a resource to help teach children. If, at the same time, you provide retired people a chance to be of service, you have actually benefited two groups.

How to start is usually the first question facing a school. Some districts hire a person, not necessarily a certificated teacher, to set up and coordinate the program. Our district has such a person, but if we didn't, we could have organized within our school with the assistance of the parent organization. One parent working cooperatively with the principal and the faculty can start a resource program in a matter of weeks. Since the program involves the school community and that means communication, the school's newspaper editor may be the most likely parent to head the effort.

Begin by organizing resources. To gather the information we needed, we sent the following letter and questionnaire home with each child:

Dear Greenwood Parents:
  Hopefully you have already heard something about Cherry Creek School District's Community Resources Program, a volunteer program of citizens of the community who have a talent, special interest, or area of expertise

which they are willing to share with school children. We know that our community contains a wealth of untapped resources that could serve to enrich our educational program, so we are asking each family to fill out this questionnaire in order to establish a catalog of people, places, and programs available to our students and teachers.

The following are a few examples of requests from Greenwood teachers for supplemental information last year: electricity, legislative process, Eskimos, drugs, forest rangers.

The purpose of this questionnaire is to discover what volunteers might be available for our talent pool—people who are interested in contributing to the education of our school children.

Please understand that returning this questionnaire does *not* constitute a commitment. You will be contacted concerning specifics when and if your specialty is requested.

PLEASE COMPLETE THIS QUESTIONNAIRE AND RETURN IT TO THE SCHOOL.

NAME_____

ADDRESS_____

PHONE_____

If you know of others who will not receive this questionnaire, but who might be interested and have something to contribute, please list their names, addresses, phone number, and contribution. We will contact them to request their help.

1. Can you help enrich children's backgrounds in the study of other countries, or sections of the United States, by sharing your experiences? If so, what countries or sections?

   Do you have slides or movies? Other materials?

2. Do you have a particular knowledge of, information on, or materials that would help children appreciate life in the past or cultural or ethnic differences (e.g., antiques, Indian artifacts, Civil War, or religious items.)?

3. Are there phases of your occupation which you could share? If so, what is your occupation?

4. Do you have a hobby or talent to share?

arts	cooking	gardening
crafts	mountaineering	collections
music	nature	(rocks, fossils,
drama	antiques	butterflies,
carpentry	sports	etc.)
woodworking	animals	

Others:_____

5. Do you have something to contribute in other areas of interest? (Human relations, the community, science, other?) Please specify.

6. Would you be interested in helping in the classroom if extra help is needed for a project?

If you have volunteered your service to the school in this questionnaire would you be available for:

Greenwood only_____
All Cherry Creek Schools_____
Elementary_____
Middle (Jr. High)_____
Senior High_____

THANK YOU FOR YOUR TIME AND HELP!!!

Besides surveying the parent population, contact community organizations, such as Kiwanis, Elks Club, American Legion, NAACP, and others, by mail, telling them what you are doing and asking their help. Put notices in the local paper and ask interested individuals to contact the school. Ask all who inquire to fill out a questionnaire. When questionnaires are in, enlist volunteer help to verify each one through a phone call to make certain the person is as represented and genuinely willing to help.

Then use the information to compile a Community Resource Catalog, in the form of a loose leaf notebook. We divide our catalog into major subject headings, such as Creative Art, and file a one-page summary of each resource in the appropriate category under the major subject heading. Field trip information is also included. Samples of summary sheets follow:

FIELD TRIPS: Science

RESOURCE: Denver Botanical Gardens
909 York
297-2547

CONTACT PERSON: Margaret Sikes, Education
Director

GRADE LEVEL: 4–12

TIME NEEDED: One hour

SIZE OF GROUP: 60 children—1 adult for
every 10

EXPENSES:

AVAILABILITY: 9:30 Wednesday and
Thursday
10:30 Tuesday and
Thursday
Two weeks' notice

SPECIAL NEEDS:

ADDITIONAL
INFORMATION: The guided tour usually
explains plants in the
conservatory highlighting
commercial plants like
coffee, bananas, etc. The
tours can be adapted to
whatever is of particular
interest. Fall and winter are
excellent times to go. The
Gardens lend themselves to
visits from art students.

DATED
8–72

CREATIVE ART: Crafts

RESOURCE:	Dan Myers Blue Bottle Tree Larimer Square 1420 Larimer 825-6403
OCCUPATION:	Glass cutter
GRADE LEVEL:	
LENGTH OF PROGRAM:	
SIZE OF GROUP:	
EXPENSES:	
AVAILABILITY:	The shop and all work is done by two people—their availability depends upon how busy they are.
SPECIAL NEEDS:	
DESCRIPTION OF RESOURCE:	Dan Myers would be happy to do a glass cutting demonstration as his time allows.
DATED 9–72	

The district's community resource director prepared the following guidelines for teacher use. Guidelines in the beginning help prevent problems later.

GUIDELINES FOR USING COMMUNITY RESOURCES

Please follow these guidelines:

1. *Call the resource to set a date.*
   The original contact may have been made as many as several months earlier, and the resource may need to be

refreshed. Discuss the particular aspect of his subject in which your class is interested, how familiar the class is with the subject, the length of the program, and whether such materials as a projector, blackboards, or tables need to be on hand.

2. *Prepare your class.*
   Consider such questions as why you are inviting this resource, what you want to find out, when questions should be asked and how the answers can be remembered, and how shall the class act while the guest is there.

3. *Inform the school secretary and other office personnel about the visit* so that the visitor may be made to feel at home.

4. *Notify the Community Resource Program Office.*
   If it is a first time visitor to our district, the director would like to be there in order to help evaluate the resource. This is also one way to keep track of which resources go to which schools and to avoid overworking them.

5. *Try to be flexible enough so that the students are prepared for the visitor but not sitting and waiting so that they get impatient in case the visitor is late.*
   Resource people have responsibilities and obligations outside of our schools, and may not be familiar with the area, and they may be late on occasion.

6. *Please remember that the classroom teacher is, and should remain, in charge of the class.*
   Disciplining, watching time and sometimes helping to direct discussion is the responsibility of the teacher. Most resource people have had no training in teaching techniques.

7. *After the resource has visited, a thank you is in order.*
   Either a class-dictated letter or individual ones might be sent. These are really appreciated.

8. *Please fill out the evaluation form and send it to this office.*
   We need your help and ideas in developing a really great program!

Keep the catalog in a central location such as the teachers' reference section of the library so it will be handy for teachers to use. Tape a pocket for evaluation forms, such as the following, to the inside cover of the catalog and ask teachers to fill out a form and send it to a central file for future reference each time they use a resource.

COMMUNITY RESOURCE EVALUATION FORM

Please fill out and return immediately after resource has visited. Return to: Helene Linkon, Community Resource Program, Teachers' Center, Holly Ridge School.

RESOURCE: _____SUBJECT: _____

SCHOOL:_____TEACHER:_____DATE:_____

GRADE LEVEL: ____NUMBER OF STUDENTS PARTICIPATING:____

How was the resource used?   *Excellent Good Fair Poor*

Introduction & motivation for unit study_____
Presentation of basic information for unit study_____
Culmination or review of unit study_____
Supplementary information of unit study_____
Demonstration of a skill_____
Other (explain)_____
Promptness_____
Presentation of subject_____
Knowledge of subject_____
Communication with students_____
Value of content_____

- - - - - - - - - - - - - -

What preparation do you suggest prior to visit?_____

_____

Would you recommend this resource or use it again?
___yes ___no
Additional comments:_____

_____

_____

BUDGETS AND FUNDS FOR TODAY'S SCHOOL

"From Dollars to Doughnuts"
❖❖❖❖❖

TWENTY YEARS AGO IN A SCHOOL DISTRICT IN IDAHO, THE superintendent sent his secretary around to the different schools to distribute the supplies he had decided they should have. When teachers joked with others in the system because the secretary counted out one red pencil for each teacher for the year, one who had been there a long time said, "Don't laugh. They used to break them in half."

With all the new equipment and special programs necessary for schools today, a superintendent could hardly get away with allocating supplies that way. Budgets are becoming increasingly complex, and as they do, superintendents are delegating some of the responsibility for their preparation to the principals. This makes sense, for each school is unique. The principal is in a position to know what his school needs and is able to involve his staff in budgeting to meet those needs.

◆ CREATING A DECENTRALIZED SCHOOL BUDGET

Five years ago our principals and superintendent discussed budget problems at an administrative meeting. They decided the district would allocate a certain amount of money, based on student enrollment projections for the coming year, to each school. The principal and his staff, instead of the central office, would determine how that money would be spent. Principals sought control over spending in their buildings to further the district goal of individualizing instruction.

Principals and the superintendent identified and, with the board's approval, decentralized budget items that applied to the operation of the individual schools. Seventeen items were on the list: textbooks, library books, encyclopedia replacements, remedial reading, magazines, audiovisual materials and supplies, teaching supplies, office supplies, convention travel, office equipment, curriculum study, in-service training, equipment replacements, new school equipment, student activities, audiovisual equipment, and library equipment.

Money for staff was decentralized too but in a different way. Each school is allowed so many teacher spaces, depending upon the number of students. Cost of a teacher space is figured on the basis of the average teacher salary in the district. Therefore, if we want to pay a team leader above the salary schedule or hire aides and interns rather than a teacher, money available is based on that average salary. Teacher salaries are paid out of the district budget according to the salary schedule, and it doesn't affect an individual school budget if teachers are above or below average on the district salary scale.

Not all budget items were decentralized (teacher salaries, capital construction, and capital outlay among them), mainly because they would be too complicated and time consuming for the principals to handle.

Principals did not want to do all of their own ordering either, for they didn't have the clerical help to do it; so the district keeps each school's money in a separate account. Requisitions for supplies are still sent through the central office and approved as a matter of formality. They are routinely filled and paid from the school's account.

Personnel expenditures are handled another way. For instance, teacher travel money is paid by the business office out of the school's fund after the principal authorizes reimbursement. We have a form for this purpose, and the same form is used to transfer money from the school's account to the district substitute account when we hire substitutes for teachers doing in-service work or attending in-service meetings or workshops.

GREENWOOD SCHOOL
AUTHORIZATION OF BUDGET TRANSFER

TO: Director of business office

FROM: Principal _____
                              SIGNATURE

DATE:

Please charge the following to Greenwood's decentralized budget account.

$ _____ Amount

_____ Account number

REASON _____

_____

_____

_____

(FOR TRAVEL ONLY)
Send reimbursement checks to:

NAME	MILEAGE
NAME	MILEAGE
NAME	MILEAGE

Decentralized budget requires record keeping in the school office. A ledger book like those used by accountants or bookkeepers is handy to have. We record each budget item under a separate heading and include the amount budgeted. When we make an expenditure, we record the amount under the appropriate heading. Periodic checks keep us informed about the state of the account.

The budget shows a dollar figure for each of the seventeen items. However, there is no rule that the money must be spent in those categories. For example, if $700 is allocated for equipment replacements, and it turns out that only $300 is needed, we transfer the money to another item where we may need to spend more, such as teaching supplies. The decision is up to the school.

To encourage innovation, one principal sets aside $2,000 for teachers wanting to try something new. They submit proposals, and he allocates the money if he feels the project is worthy.

◆ INVOLVING STAFF IN BUDGET PLANNING AND SPENDING

Once the school budget is decentralized, the principal can go a step further and let the unit leaders and the special teachers decide how their money will be spent. When teachers draw up their own budgets, they have no grounds for complaint, and it is one less thing for the principal to do.

In our building unit leaders plan with their teams, but they are responsible for funds set aside for their unit. A committee composed of all unit leaders and the principal makes spending decisions that affect more than one team.

The librarian, music teacher, physical education teacher, and guidance counselor all have allocations. They are responsible for those funds, but in all cases the principal has final authority to authorize requisitions.

It seems teachers are more careful about spending when the money comes out of a budget for which they are responsible. If they order from one vast, seemingly unlimited district fund, they feel no restraints and want all kinds of things. However, when they work with their own figures, they see what the limitations are. They figure their money down to the last penny. One team leader came into the office upset because her team requisitions came to $1.58 more than its budget allowed. She was relieved when told that the school budget could make up the difference.

The first year we planned our own budget, we sent budget planning forms similar to requisition forms and the following letter to grade-level chairmen, and library, physical education, and music teachers:

> We need to develop an estimate of projected costs in order to effectively budget our allocated funds. Your help in working with fellow teachers to determine these needs is most important.
>
> It is anticipated that your requests will amount to more than our allotted funds. Therefore, we will need to determine priority after this first planning stage.
>
> The office will assume responsibility for estimating previous cost needs in such categories as: office supplies, teaching supplies, blue card items, and workbooks. You will be responsible for estimating needs in the areas of textbooks, library equipment, library books, audiovisual materials, new equipment, field trips, audiovisual equipment, furniture and shelving, physical education supplies and equipment, music equipment and supplies.
>
> Please list items on the attached pages and return to the office by April 18th.

Since that time we have refined the form and defined roles to the point where people can easily see where spending authority for each item lies. A copy follows:

GREENWOOD SCHOOL
BUDGET—1973
Spending Authority—Principal

AMOUNT BUDGETED	ITEM CATEGORY	RECOM-MENDING PERSON	EXPLANATION
$ 2,500.00	Textbooks	Unit leaders	Priority established through unit leaders and subject area committee's recommendation.

AMOUNT BUDGETED	ITEM CATEGORY	RECOM-MENDING PERSON	EXPLANATION
1,200.00	Library books	Librarian/ Media	Teachers and unit leaders make recommendations to librarian.
110.00	Encyclopedias	Librarian/ Media	Replace one classroom set.
106.00	Remedial reading	Unit leaders	Purchase teaching materials, books, or supplies for Right to Read Program.
671.00	Magazines and nonbooks	Librarian/ Media	Teachers and unit leaders make recommendations to librarian.
575.00	A–V materials and supplies	Librarian/ Media	Teachers and unit leaders make specific recommendations for filmstrips, tapes, overhead materials, and all related A–V supplies. Librarian's responsibility to coordinate this category with faculty.
5,000.00	Teaching supplies	Principal/ School secretary	School secretary responsible for keeping supplies ordered. Includes ditto paper, art supplies, pencils, chalk, etc.
2,000.00	Teaching supplies	Unit leaders	Mostly consumable items such as workbooks, commercial tests, newspapers, etc. Priority established through unit leaders meeting with the principal.

AMOUNT BUDGETED	ITEM CATEGORY	RECOMMENDING PERSON	EXPLANATION
1,373.00	Office supplies	Principal/ School secretary	Secretary's responsibility to keep principal informed of needs by writing requisitions for his approval. Items for office use only.
513.00	Convention travel	Unit leaders	Committee decision— requests must be submitted one month in advance.
275.00	Miscellaneous office	Principal	Equipment items for office.
700.00	Curriculum improvement	Unit leaders	Priority established through unit leaders and subject area committee's recommendations.
700.00	In-service training	Unit leaders	Unit leaders make recommendation along with principal's staff development plans.
400.00	Equipment replacement	Principal	Principal's decision based on unit leaders' recommendations.
615.00	Student activity	Unit leaders	Mostly field trips. Field trip requests must be signed by the unit leader and the principal.
1,733.00	Equipment for the school	Principal/ Unit leaders	New equipment such as student furniture or playground equipment.
700.00	A–V equipment	Librarian/ Media	Teachers and unit leaders make specific recommendations to librarian for such items as tape recorders, record players, etc.

AMOUNT BUDGETED	ITEM CATEGORY	RECOM- MENDING PERSON	EXPLANATION
231.00	Library equipment	Librarian/ Media	For furniture, and specific items for the library and media center.

Special Categories

400.00	Music & Physical Education	Teachers	Teachers decide how this money is spent based on projected needs.
50.00	Health room	Secretary/ Nurse	Band-aids, etc.
50.00	Band & Orchestra	Teacher	Supplies such as sheet music.
739.17	Unit/grade level Kg & 1	Unit leader A	Unit leaders plan with their teams in spending these funds. Amount in this category is based on projected unit enrollment multiplied by $5.73. The total amount planned for this category was approximately $3,771.00.
538.62	Unit/grade level 2	Unit leader B9	
595.92	Unit/grade level 3	Unit leader C	
538.62	Unit/grade level 4	Unit leader D	
653.22	Unit/grade level 5	Unit leader E	
704.79	Unit/grade level 6	Unit leader F	
200.00	Guidance & counseling	Teacher	For equipment and supplies for the counseling program.
1,000.00	Reserve for emergencies	Principal	For new programs and unexpected costs.

Total Budget

$24,873.00

◆ PLANNING WITH THE CENTRAL OFFICE

An item such as carpeting for the library and media center would not be included in our decentralized budget because it would come under capital outlay. If we want such an item, we must plan with the central office. Presenting a dream list isn't the answer. There must be an educationally sound reason behind each request. We may justify the carpeting, for example, by showing that it will increase student use and further individualization by cutting down the noise of children working in groups.

When writing proposals that require additional funds, we find it helpful to follow six basic rules:

1. Start planning at least one year in advance.

2. Form a faculty committee and involve it from start to finish. Include a member of the parent organization for certain proposals such as playground equipment.

3. Present information such as test results and other data in your proposal to back up your statements.

4. Show a definite deadline date on budget requests.

5. Itemize costs.

6. Show how you will evaluate the program. Be specific about the criteria or materials you will use.

In Colorado district budgets go into effect January 1 and run through December 31. Since we know our budget allocation in January, we plan and make expenditures accordingly. If there is not enough money to meet a request from the current budget, the request is carried over to the next year. Recommendations go to the superintendent's office prior to initial preparation of the district budget in August.

◆ THE INDEPENDENT SCHOOL FUND

A school fund, independent of district or parent organization funds, finances special school projects and activities.

Ours is created largely through a small return on student purchases. For instance, school photographers, at least in this area, who take individual and class pictures, give the schools a slight percentage of their profits. This goes into the fund as does money earned from paper, pen, and pencil vending machines in the hall. Miscellaneous money, such as parent donations not marked for special purposes, is another source, although not a major source of income.

We call our fund the Greenwood School Fund and have a bank checking account under that name. The principal is directly responsible for the account, and checks carry his signature, even though the bank also has the assistant superintendent's signature on record just in case.

The fund is convenient for teachers because they can turn in book or magazine money that they've collected from students, and we issue a check to the company drawn on the school fund. This way they don't have to write personal checks. They are protected, and the school is protected.

Since most of the money comes from the children, we try to return it to them in one way or another. Movies, supplies for school programs, a bowling party for students going on to the middle school, a class project, or a tree for the outdoor learning lab are all legitimate uses for fund money. One year we added fund money to parent organization and school board funds to purchase a public address system. Children benefited indirectly since it is used to send them messages they need to receive.

We are particularly careful about this account since the principal has direct access to the fund and is responsible for it. Receipts and checks that account for every expenditure and a once-a-year audit prevent problems.

◆ FUND RAISING AND THE PARENT ORGANIZATION

Although the primary objective of the parent-teacher organization should be cooperation between the two groups rather than fund raising, most organizations put more effort into fund raising. However, when teachers and parents work together on a project, more cooperation results, so perhaps the money raising meets the primary objective in a round-about way.

An organization working to do something for the school should include teachers and the principal in planning the fund raising activity and in decisions regarding items to be purchased with the money raised. Unless teachers express a need for a specific item, the organization might be wasting its time raising money to buy it for them.

When a committee of parents and teachers set purchase priorities early in the year and work toward that goal, it is more likely to gain cooperation from other parents and to purchase items satisfactory to both groups. One year our committee decided to improve the outdoor learning lab and to purchase some audiovisual equipment and a laminator for the school. Through the school paper, parents were made aware of the priorities, and later, after the money had been raised and spent, the committee gave an accounting.

Fund raising activities can be an educational experience as well as fun for children and should be planned to include them. Several activities we have used successfully are:

◇   A school supply store, open before school on Mondays, Wednesdays, and Fridays. Children run the store under parent supervision, making sales, change, and taking inventory.

◇   Bake sales. Children and parents make cookies, cakes, doughnuts, and even bake bread for the bake sale. Since our school is a polling place, bake sales held during elections were most successful.

◇   Cookbook sales. *The Greenwood Gourmet* sold widely and included many student recipes.

◇   School carnival. Always a big family affair and fund raiser. Children help organize, contribute ideas, run booths, and conduct games.

◇   School directory. Published early in the school year and sold to parents. Children help alphabetize cards containing family names, addresses, and phone numbers.

ESTABLISHING
A COUNSELING PROGRAM

"An Ounce of Prevention"
❖❖❖❖

"AN OUNCE OF PREVENTION IS WORTH A POUND OF CURE" IS AN old adage that applies to new counseling programs. Counseling has been and still is commonly reserved for the junior and senior high school where "problems" are referred to a counselor. An increasing number of elementary schools, however, are adding a full-time counselor to their staffs because we now know that early attention to adjustment needs of the young child positively contributes to the adjustment of the adult he is to become.

There is some question as to whether teachers alone can carry on a counseling program, and some still insist there is no need for a specially trained, full-time counselor. Overwhelming evidence, though, indicates that the efforts of teachers alone fall far short of a program with a full-time staff counselor.

For one thing, teachers do not have enough time to do all the counseling that needs to be done. For another, many teachers lack the training.

This doesn't mean that all counseling should be left to the counselor. Attention to the needs and welfare of the individual child is a basic part of good teaching, but the teacher alone cannot take the place of a staff counselor.

◆ EMPLOYING A FULL-TIME ELEMENTARY COUNSELOR

Two problems that face a staff trying to establish a counseling program are financing and location. The expense involved is mainly that of the counselor's salary. The Greenwood staff solved this problem by agreeing (they signed a letter to this effect) to give up one teacher space for the counseling position. With a staff of twenty-five teachers, this meant increasing the class ratio approximately one student per class.

Although no elaborate set-up or specially built space is necessary, you do need a room to accommodate a counseling program. Most older schools do not have a counseling room because, until recently, counseling in the elementary school was not common.

The room (consider it a room, not an office) should measure about 10 x 14 feet. It is best not to locate the counseling room too near the principal's office, but you may have to to find the space. Look around your building. If you have a large office with unused space, partition part of it for the counseling room, convert a storeroom you no longer use, or empty an audiovisual room by dispersing equipment to instructional areas.

We used a room originally planned for instrument practice. We moved the practice program to the gym and converted the instrument room to the counseling room.

Wherever you put it, think of the counseling room as one of the most valuable instructional areas in the school. It is valuable because, while it provides the necessary privacy for counseling sessions and for parent-teacher-child conferences, a child's attitudes about himself can be changed here.

◆ COUNSELING PROGRAM PROPOSAL

Most counseling programs start with a proposal to the school board. Our proposal, which may be of help to others, follows:

NEED

Our schools today pay eloquent lip service to the concepts of development of moral and ethical values in children; helping each child grow to his fullest potential; growth in all aspects of personality including mental, physical, social, and emotional development; and fulfilling the individual's need to solve his own problems and thus continue his task of building a satisfying self-concept. Yet, no one person on the staff of the school and no one aspect of the curriculum is devoted to any highly specific concern with the moral, ethical, social, emotional, personal problem-solving, or self-concept development of the child. The affective domain plays second fiddle to mental and physical development. Growth in the affective domain is a concomitant learning process, and we assume that it is proceeding in a healthy way. Clearly, there is a place in our school today for a guidance counselor, a person whose major concern is the affective development of the children of the school.

PURPOSE

The major purpose of the guidance and counseling program should be to focus on the affective domain so that interests, attitudes, values, and appreciations as well as growth in social, emotional, and self-realization aspects of the children's lives can be facilitated to a greater degree than is now possible. To accomplish this purpose, the counselor must necessarily focus on all aspects of counseling: remedial, preventive, and promotional. In remedial counseling the counselor works with children who have problems; in preventive counseling the counselor works with individuals to try to ward off possible or probable problems; and in promotional counseling the counselor seeks to strengthen and support an effective learning climate in the school.

OBJECTIVES

The specific objectives of this counseling program would be: (1) to try to meet the unique affective needs of the children on a highly individualized basis and *(2)* to work with staff members to improve and enrich the learning climate in the school by maintaining open channels of communication among teachers, children, parents, and interested others.

To achieve these objectives the counseling program will focus on developmental, personal, and social counseling. The basic premises underlying this choice of direction are that *(1)* the child has the potential for growth in a positive direction, and *(2)* the child lives in a social environment including family, teachers, peers, and interested others.

PROCESS

The usual mode of operation would be to work with children on an individual basis or in small groups. The counselor would rarely work with class-sized groups. The counselor would work with teachers individually or in groups as needs might dictate. The counselor would be available to confer with staff members, principal, nurse, speech therapist, aides, cooks, janitors, parents, and interested others as needs might arise.

The counseling program would be organized so that any interested person could refer a child to the counselor. There would be procedures established for self-referrals and teacher-referrals. Referrals from interested others would be handled in whatever way might be appropriate at the time of the referral.

The preferred method of operation would be to talk with the child first. In many cases talks with the child might continue over a period of time. In the majority of instances, this first step would also be the last. In a minority of instances the succeeding steps would be to: *(2)* talk with interested others, *(3)* test to discover other problems such as a reading deficiency or a learning disability, *(4)* confer about the test results with the interested others, *(5)* hold a staff meeting concerning the child. It should be noted that this sequence might be broken and/or terminated after any step if the problems appeared to be solved at that point.

Because of the personal nature of much of the communication with the counselor, confidentiality is a prime requisite of an effective counseling program. The counselor would ask the understanding and patience of all concerned when the confidentiality of a client must be respected.

ROLE

The role of the counselor is threefold: (1) counselor, (2) consultant, and (3) coordinator. The counselor works with children individually or in small groups to free the normal growth and developmental processes in the life of the child. As a consultant, the counselor works with others, usually teachers and/or parents, to gain deeper insight into the development of the child. The sharing of information is mutual and extends from teachers to counselor as well as from counselor to teachers. The role of coordinator is usually filled only by a full-time counselor. As a coordinator, the counselor has the responsibility of coordinating all the pupil personnel services of the school into a pattern meaningful to the development of the particular child under consideration.

The role of the teacher in the counseling program is also threefold: (1) observation, (2) cooperation, and (3) participation. The teacher is sensitive to the affective needs and developmental patterns of the children and refers them to the counselor when the need is there. The teacher permits the counselor to take children from the classroom for individual or small group counseling and also permits the counselor to observe a child in the classroom when necessary. The teacher participates in conferences about the child initiated by others and also initiates discussion about children and their related problems of growth and development.

The role of the principal can also be considered threefold: (1) facilitator, (2) participator, and (3) provider. The principal encourages a cooperative working relationship among teachers, parents, and the counselor. The principal participates in conferences with the counselor and with interested others when the need arises. The principal provides adequate space for counseling and adequate equipment to meet the needs of the counseling program.

EVALUATION

Because of the highly subjective nature of the counseling program, evaluation must necessarily be more subjective than objective. It is proposed that evaluation be made informally by keeping a record of the statements made by interested persons about the value of the counseling program throughout the year. A somewhat more formal evaluation should be made in February or March by opinionnaire. This opinionnaire should have two purposes: *(1)* to assess the value of the counseling program both to individuals and to the school as a whole and *(2)* to provide suggestions for improving the program if it is deemed worthy of being continued.

♦ HOW THE COUNSELOR FUNCTIONS AS A COUNSELOR, CONSULTANT, AND COORDINATOR

Our proposal stated that the counselor's role would be three-fold. He would counsel, consult, and coordinate. In the first role, that of counselor, he would meet with students on a one-to-one basis or in small groups to counsel with them. The proposal also stated that in addition to referrals by others for counseling purposes, there would be procedures established for self-referrals.

In actual practice, we placed boxes that looked like valentine boxes in the school library, the office, the cafeteria, and the classrooms, wherever students congregated. Students could write a note to the counselor and drop it in the box. We wondered at the time whether or not the students would take advantage of this opportunity to get in touch with the counselor. The self-referrals, however, have turned out to be one of the most effective parts of our program. The counselor finds notes written on gum wrappers (although we have a no gum-chewing policy), on notebook pages, or on torn scraps of paper.

Through self-referrals, one counselor uncovered a major social problem in his school. The students referred themselves and came to see the counselor. He listened to the students express their anger and watched them take out their hostilities on a punching bag. As he watched and listened, he realized much of the anger was directed toward the same students. These students were the gym class captains, who had influence over the other students, not only during play time but in the classroom as well. There was a leader hierarchy, and it was causing problems. In his role as coordinator, the counselor alerted the staff to the problem, and together they worked toward a solution.

You may wonder about the punching bag. Although opinions vary among counselors as to what specific items will help the most in their work with children, a punching bag, a peopled and furnished doll house, toy animals, and toy guns are all items that counselors use to help children express their feelings. For example, through the doll house medium, a child expresses his relationship with his family. As he plays with the dolls, he reveals his feelings toward his brothers, sisters, mother, and father. Once the counselor understands the child's real feelings, he is better able to help the child solve his home or school problems.

As a consultant, the counselor serves as a resource person for the staff. Meeting with teacher teams or individual teachers, the counselor helps them understand not only the children they teach but their own teaching behavior. Discussion topics might range from positive reinforcement as a teaching technique, to ways children learn and group activities that promote acceptance of others. In a consultant role, our counselor arranged a workshop on affective education for the staff.

Parents, too, are receptive to advice that the counselor, as a consultant, offers. Some counselors write a column in the school paper, discussing some aspect of student behavior. The following from a column called "The Counselor's Corner" is an example:

> Teasing is a way of expressing anger. Are your children giving or getting too much anger/teasing? This is frequently a very distressing problem for children because they do not know alternative ways of handling these difficult and troublesome emotions.
>
> We believe that both children and adults will experience much less confusion and hostility if they can learn to express their angry feelings more directly, and also to deal with direct rather than indirect (teasing) expressions of anger.
>
> A problem, in order to be a problem, has to cause problems. If teasing is a problem in your household and you would like help on how to deal with this in your specific situation, we would be happy to do what we can to help you to understand the dynamics of the angry situations and find more appropriate ways to deal with the very strong feelings involved.

The third role of the counselor, that of a coordinator who coordinates the child's school life with his home and community life into a meaningful pattern of development, can begin each year with the new student orientation. The counselor comes to know new students and parents as he contacts them about the orientation program. He arranges for older students to serve as guides while new students tour the building, for the counselor realizes that a young student who knows his way around and sees a familiar face won't feel so lost his first day in a new school.

Since the counselor is a coordinator, he must keep parents informed of the counseling program. Articles in the school paper and letters to parents keep the lines of communication open. Our counselor wrote the following letter to the parents of our school:

Dear Parents:

As most of you know, the counseling program is moving into its second year. We hope that you consider this an advantage to your child. Our major focus has not changed —we will still be largely concerned with the affective development of the children. Their feelings, emotions, likes, dislikes, interests, and values have such an important role in their motivation and hence in their learning that we feel it advisable to let them know that we care about this aspect of their growth.

The self-referral concept was so well received by the children last year that our decision is to continue it for this year. Of course, we will also see those children who are referred by their teachers or by their parents. In addition to seeing children who have been referred to us, some of our time is spent working with parents, teachers, and other school personnel. It is our hope that this expenditure of time will lead to a more effective learning climate for every child.

As always, one of our major aims is to increase the communication between parents, teachers, and children. Therefore, you may rest assured that we will be in contact with you about our work when it involves your child in a counseling-type situation. As you probably realize, the counselor is considered a teacher, too, and when our contact with the child is in the nature of a teacher-child contact, we would not necessarily contact you any more than any other teacher would.

We hope to have a regular column in the paper to keep you apprised of what's new in the counseling room. We have but one favor to ask of the parents: *Please* give us a call if something seems to be going amiss. It is much easier to solve little potential problems than to try to solve old long-standing ones.

We hope to be hearing from you soon. The counseling room is located in the short hall between rooms 7 and 9. Stop by if you have time.

These few examples of the counselor in action don't begin to cover all that a counselor does or deals with. The counselor often sponsors the student council. He orders counseling kits and shows and discusses the filmstrips the kits contain. He does shadow studies of students where he observes a child on the playground, in the classroom, in the lunchroom, and even coming or going to and from school. He is in contact with mental health agencies. He keeps records.

Counselors should not necessarily do the same things. The counselor's job—like the counseling program—is individual, designed to meet the needs of the school and the community. But even though the job is individual, the goal is common—trying to solve little problems before they become big ones.

NEW INSTRUMENTS
FOR DEVELOPMENT
AND EVALUATION

"Blueprints and Yardsticks"
❖❖❖❖

AT AN ELEMENTARY PRINCIPALS' MEETING THERE WAS SOME discussion of the Individually Guided Education Program. One principal said he had heard of schools that had belonged to IGE, but the program didn't work for them. Another man, a principal of an IGE school, said, "It's a good program. If it didn't work, the people who tried to implement it failed—not the program. They just didn't try hard enough to make it go." Perhaps there were other reasons, but it is true that the success or failure of the new programs depends largely upon the people involved.

It is not easy to implement new programs. It is easier to do nothing. Even one change such as going from a self-contained classroom to a team teaching situation takes work and commitment, but going into a totally new school program such as IGE takes even more. Why do it at all then? is the question. To improve instruction is the answer.

◆ INDIVIDUALLY GUIDED EDUCATION

A school that has successfully implemented some of the new approaches might be ready for more and should consider joining one of the programs designed to help. We joined and are most familiar with the Individually Guided Education Program developed by the Wisconsin Research and Development Center for Cognitive Learning, the Institute for Development of Educational Activities, Inc., and cooperating educational institutions.

IGE provides elementary schools with a framework for individualizing instruction. Features include the learning cycle; student, teacher, and parent decision-making; a wide choice of methods and materials to encourage self-directed learning; a home-school communication program; Leagues of Cooperating Schools, which meet for support and idea sharing; and alternative courses of action.

The program appealed to us in the first place because it could be implemented in traditionally built as well as in open space schools. It seemed a logical way to bring about change. It offered a total systems approach to managing a school, that is, it included everything from in-service training to evaluation. Finally, we were impressed by the fact that the program had been field tested, so that what had worked in another school could be adapted to work for us, and we didn't have to "reinvent the wheel."

There are several ways to join IGE. One way is to begin by being an observer school. While taking part in other IGE schools' activities, such as attending meetings or sending teachers to visit, and while implementing what you want to implement without being committed, you can see whether the program offers what you really want. This is the method recommended by the IGE developers.

A second way is to hit it straight on, that is, sign a commitment and join the program. It is not really practical though to jump into a complete program without getting your feet wet in preliminary programs. The change is too drastic and too disconcerting to teachers trying to do too many new things at once. We don't recommend this approach, as we know of no school that adopted the program all at once that lasted as an IGE school.

The third way is to do as we did. Our school philosophy fitted the IGE philosophy, and our teaching approach was similar to the learning cycle proposed by IGE. We were even organized in teams much as the IGE model. We made a few changes to fit the IGE program, but because we already had so much in common with IGE, it was easy to go into the program without becoming an observer school.

At the time some of the faculty asked why we needed to join a program if we were doing the same things. A Colorado State Department of Education orientation showed us why. We saw that the IGE program could further improve instruction, improve staff in-service, involve the staff in decision-making, and give a stamp of creditability to what we were already doing.

Our whole approach, and maybe the key to implementing IGE (or any new program for that matter), was "don't sweat it." In other words, don't let some minor detail of the program interfere with the overall goal. Since no two elementary schools are exactly alike, and yet IGE is a design for all schools, different schools will implement the program in their own ways. For example, one component of IGE is the organizational pattern for grouping students for learning. IGE suggests multi-age grouping. Each school has a different student body make-up and reasons to group different ways, and this is all right.

IGE has a blueprint to follow, but there is flexibility within the blueprint. There is no set way of doing things. Changes can be made to meet your school's individual needs. Just as there are several ways to reach the top of Pike's Peak (you can take a car, a bus, the cograil, hike the trails, come by helicopter, or parachute down), there are several ways to implement an IGE program.

In the *IGE Implementation Guide* the developers describe their program as a "proven method of creating a relaxed personalized environment that is highly conducive to learning—an environment that 'turns children on, not off.'" This may be what a principal meant when he commented that he didn't know for certain that the children were learning more, but he did know that since his school had gone into IGE, students who had been absent more than they were present were coming every day.

You may obtain further information about IGE by writing the Wisconsin Research and Development Center for Cognitive Learning, 1404 Regent Street, Madison, Wisconsin 53706, or by contacting I/D/E/A (Institute for Development of Educational Activities), 5335 Far Hills Avenue, Dayton, Ohio 45429.

◆ PROGRAM EVALUATION

Before beginning any new program, particularly one as sweeping as IGE, you need to know how you are going to evaluate it. Evaluation is as important as implementation. You need to know whether or not the new is any better or even as good as the old. Besides, honest evaluation leads to improvement.

The public, partly because it continually puts more and more tax money into the schools, wants proof of results. Accountability demands that schools account for what they are doing; evaluation to determine whether goals have been met is the only way to tell.

To evaluate a program, you should have a plan. The plan need not be complicated, but it should describe what is going to be evaluated and some of the measures that will be used. We began by stating what we were trying to do:

◇   Further develop pupil progress reporting.

◇   Improve communication with parents.

◇   Identify areas of weakness and strength on which we need to focus attention.

◇   Continually evaluate and improve curriculum design and behavioral objectives.

◇   Compare our programs with current programs on local as well as national levels to determine their effectiveness in terms of pupil growth.

◇   Evaluate ourselves as to teaching abilities and methods.

◇   Upgrade the curriculum, improve facilities, and provide personnel with quality training and experience to meet children's needs in a changing world.

◇   Evaluate each student in areas of growth and improve evaluation through testing and teacher judgment.

Program evaluation must fit the current instructional program within the building. Since the program changes from year to year, so must the evaluation plan. Principal and teachers together are responsible for setting up the evaluation plan with the help of outside sources such as the central office, state department of education, or a consultant service. Outside help is recommended because no one school faculty knows everything there is to know about program evaluation. They need help with what is to be evaluated and how to go about it.

Many points have to be taken into consideration when a program is evaluated. For instance, if you have more first-year teachers than experienced teachers on your faculty, this would have an effect on the evaluation. District factors such as salary schedule, total district budget, and central office assistance all affect what you are trying to do.

There are measurement instruments outside and inside the school that you can use. We evaluate our program using some of each. Outside sources include:

◇   IGE questionnaires.

◇   *Indicators of Quality*, prepared by Associated Public School Systems, Columbia University.

◇   National standardized tests such as the Iowa Tests of Basic Skills.

◇   President's Physical Fitness Test for Boys and Girls.

◇   Evaluation reports from outside consultants.

◇   Written evaluations from out-of-district visitors.

◇ Publisher-designed reading tests, including comparisons with national norms.

Evaluation instruments within the school include:

◇ Oral and written student surveys.

◇ Teacher surveys.

◇ *"33" Roles for Teachers and Pupils in the Classroom*, prepared by Associated Public School Systems, Columbia University.

◇ Oral and written teacher tests for student evaluation.

A standardized achievement test might measure skills, but it won't measure attitudes or how well you are doing in regard to individualizing instruction or fostering creativity in your students. This is why when it comes to evaluation, you must go beyond achievement tests and measure your program in relation to your goals.

◆ INDICATORS OF QUALITY

Indicators of Quality, often referred to as "Indicators," is a measuring instrument devised by the Associated Public School Systems (APSS), Teachers College, Columbia University. APSS is an organization to which our district belongs. We learned about "Indicators" through its literature and by talking with APSS staff consultants. We specifically mention it in our plan, because it helped us change our program through evaluation. It is an instrument that can be used by an entire school district but must be administered in individual schools.

We liked "Indicators" because it attempts to measure school quality in the areas of *(1)* individualization, *(2)* interpersonal regard, *(3)* creativity, and *(4)* group activity. These are the four areas we feel, as does APSS, are "basic to quality." The authors say the term "Indicators" was chosen advisedly; there may be other indicators of school quality, but these four are of undisputed importance.

Teams of teachers and administrators observe critical behavior within the classroom to obtain measures of school quality. There are fifty-one items to be observed—seventeen regarding teacher behavior, seventeen regarding pupil behavior, and seventeen regarding interaction between teachers and pupils. All items relate to the four indicators.

Part of the evaluation procedure is to observe specific classroom activities in terms of positive or negative factors. For example, on the positive side under interpersonal regard would be the fact that the teacher is cheerful and pleasant. A negative factor would be that the teacher appears discontented and cross. Classroom activities are specified because "Indicators" is not a teacher evaluation device.

Some teachers felt threatened though, and this seemed a natural reaction since three people were visiting and evaluating their classrooms. Once they understood that it was impossible to identify teachers on evaluation score sheets, they relaxed somewhat. No teacher was identified, and when scores came back, only school and district scores were reported.

As far as teachers were concerned, there were positive results. Administration of the instrument resulted in teacher growth, especially for those who administered it. Another benefit of the evaluations was the teacher exchange they necessitated. Those doing the evaluation did so with a cooperating district. Teachers from district A evaluated classrooms in district B, and teachers from district B evaluated classrooms in district A. Elementary teachers evaluated secondary classrooms, and secondary teachers evaluated elementary classrooms.

Scores derived from "Indicators" gave us a comparison with other district schools, the district as a whole, and other schools throughout the country who have used "Indicators." Through the evaluation we saw our weaknesses and strengths and discussed them constructively at faculty meetings.

◆ 33 ROLES FOR TEACHERS AND PUPILS IN THE CLASSROOM

33 Roles for Teachers and Pupils in the Classroom is another APSS instrument that we have found helpful. It concerns the roles of teachers and students in the classroom. The different roles, based on the same four characteristics as "Indicators," are identified in the *33 Roles* booklet. Teachers and students use their knowledge of the roles to evaluate the learning process in their own classrooms.

Because an orientation is necessary to use the *33 Roles* booklet to advantage, our school district brought in an APSS consultant for orientation purposes. He conducted a workshop for selected teachers and administrators.

Then it was up to the teachers and administrators who attended the workshop to familiarize their staffs with the workings of the instrument. Our unit leaders decided to make a videotape of a teacher teaching in a classroom situation that was as normal as possible under the circumstances. We had no trouble selecting a teacher since the one who attended the district meeting volunteered. We used the tape for faculty discussion about the thirty-three roles in the booklet.

While viewing the videotape we were able to pick out the most often observed as well as the least often observed teacher and pupil roles and to decide upon the most important teacher and pupil roles in our school. The tape provided material for meaningful discussion. Teachers then worked with their students using the booklet and the tape in the same way.

Detailed information about *Indicators of Quality* and *33 Roles for Teachers and Pupils in the Classroom* can be obtained by writing the Institute of Administrative Research, Teachers College, Columbia University, 525 West 120th Street, New York, New York, 10027.

AFTERMATH

WHEN A SCHOOL IMPLEMENTS A NEW PROGRAM, WHETHER IT involves only one change, such as using volunteers in the classroom, or a sweeping school-wide program such as IGE, the faculty is asked to change. They must change attitudes, methods, and perhaps materials. Because the new ways are not familiar, they require more preparation time, at least in the beginning, and hence a commitment on the teachers' part to be willing to work hard to make a program succeed.

The commitment, however, works both ways. The principal, sometimes to his surprise, must change too. As teachers come out of their self-contained classrooms and begin to work together, they take a more active part in decision-making. What they take, the principal must give up. He can no longer hand down decisions. He can still have a part in decision-making, but as the process changes, decisions concerning school management are not his alone.

Principals' methods of operation range from an autocratic approach where the principal lays down the rules and the teachers follow them to a total democratic approach where the principal allows the faculty to vote on all major decisions. Of course, what works in one school will not necessarily work in another, in the same way that what works for one principal will not necessarily work for another.

Principals have to operate in a way consistent with their beliefs and personality.

Because principals are different, they will not adapt to change in the same way or at the same rate, but change they must. The new programs that are freeing students are freeing faculty too—to think and act for themselves. The principal is no longer the TV or movie stereotype who disciplines the children and lectures the teachers. Rather than children being sent to the principal, the principal goes to the children, and rather than telling the teachers what to do, the principal and teachers together decide what is best.

The principal must work harder to make things happen in such a way that others may not even be aware of his influence. His satisfaction lies in seeing an idea he planted blossom into a program that improves instruction for children in his care.

ABOUT THE AUTHORS

Richard Morton is the principal of Greenwood Elementary School in the Cherry Creek School District in Colorado. He received his B.A., M.A., and Ed.D. from the University of Northern Colorado. He has organized summer workshops for elementary principals at the University of Denver and the University of Northern Colorado. During the last five years, he has served as president and state representative of the state elementary principals' organization. He is currently a member of the coordinating council of the Colorado Association of School Executives and on the board of directors of the National Association of Elementary School Principals.

An elementary principal since 1956, Dr. Morton has been with the Cherry Creek School District since 1958. Thirty years ago the district, a small rural community, still operated some one-room schoolhouses; now, due to suburban development, this is the fastest growing school district in Colorado. Cherry Creek has long been involved with innovative ideas in education. Even before innovation became a popular educational word, it had an individualized spelling and reading program. The District even operated a self-supporting farm that taught students to apply practically what they were learning about agriculture.

Four of the thirteen elementary schools in the district are new open space schools, two have been completely remodeled as open space buildings, four have been partially remodeled, and three are traditional buildings. Greenwood is a traditionally built school that hasn't undergone major renovation, but the staff is working with the latest program innovations and working toward

quality education. Greenwood School has team teaching, differentiated staffing, and individualized instruction. It is participating
in the Individually Guided Educational Program and working
with *Indicators of Quality.*

Jane Morton, who coauthored the book, earned her B.A. at
the University of Northern Colorado. She has taught for seventeen years and has had experience with the new educational
programs. In her spare time she writes for children and young
adults and has published stories and poems.

Because the authors believe that many administrators think
that the new programs will only work in the new open space
schools, they have worked together to show in this book what
can be done with the new programs within a traditional building.